THE LIFE AND TIMES OF
CRISTÓBAL COLÓN

This Book belongs to

Hollie Thompson

Hippo Books
Scholastic Children's Books
London

Scholastic Children's Books,
Scholastic Publications Ltd,
7-9 Pratt Street, London NW1 0AE, UK

Scholastic Inc.,
730 Broadway, New York, NY 10003, USA

Scholastic Canada Ltd,
123 Newkirk Road, Richmond Hill,
Ontario, Canada L4C 3G5

Ashton Scholastic Pty Ltd,
PO Box 579, Gosford, New South Wales,
Australia

Ashton Scholastic Ltd
Private Bag 1, Penrose, Auckland,
New Zealand

First published by Hippo Books 1992
An imprint of Scholastic Publications Ltd

Text copyright © 1992 by Peter Corey
Illustrations copyright © 1992 by Martin Brown

ISBN 0 590 55108 6

Typeset by Contour Typesetters, Southall, London

10 9 8 7 6 5 4 3 2 1

Five hundred years ago a brave, bold, intrepid explorer set out on a voyage of discovery. He wanted to prove that the world was flat.

It wasn't, and for all I know he is sailing still. But he need not concern us, because this book isn't about him . . .

Introduction

Cristóbal Colón? Yes! That was, believe it or not, the real name of Christopher Columbus. Now for some people a surname like Colón would be a pain in the butt, but not this guy. Oh, no! He put it behind him and did what any self-respecting young fellow might do – he ran away to sea! Fortunately he took a boat with him, or his story might have ended there, and this book would not exist.

So, what is it? Well, it's the story of Cristóbal Colón, or Christopher Columbus as we have come to know him. It is arguably the first truly faithful account of his life, from his childhood in mid-fifteenth century Genoa, via his early seafaring days, through to his accidental discovery of America.

WORLD EXCLUSIVE !!!

It may be considered an outrageous claim that this is 'arguably the first truly faithful account of his [Columbus's] life', but this claim is not made lightly. It is made with the knowledge that the information contained in this book is more accurate than any previously available, thanks to the fact that I have in my possession documentary proof of its authenticity. Documentary proof in the form of the *Colón Diaries*.

Yes, they do exist! And I will be sharing extracts from them with you through the pages of this book.

How these unique documents came into my possession is a story in itself – a story that would make the hair on the levellest head stand on end. A story that would make the hair on the baldest head grow back and then stand on end. A story that would make John le Carré's *Tinker, Tailor, Soldier, Spy* sound like a silly rhyme people say after they've eaten prunes. A story that sadly I am not at liberty to reveal, as I am honour-bound to protect my source.

Suffice it to say that dead letterboxes, under secretaries of state at foreign embassies and a second-hand underwear shop played a vital part in the securing of these diaries. Leafing through their tea-stained and type-written pages,[1] an amazing tale unfolds. A tale of long weeks on the high seas, temper-fraying tedium and cut-throat games of Travel Scrabble. The *Diaries* reveal other sides to Colón's complex, and often misunderstood, personality. For the first time we hear of his conker collection, and read the lyrics of his 1497 entry for the Eurovision Sea-Shanty Competition.

---

[1] One of the most unusual features of the diaries is that they are type-written and tea-stained. This would naturally lead some sceptics to doubt their authenticity, but to me this simply underlines just how ahead of his time Columbus was. Apart from the word processor, Colón, in collaboration with fellow seafarer Clivio Sinclari (1458 to a quarter to eleven), developed the electric car and the Speak-Your-Weight Black Forest Gateaux. The tea-staining was simply a cheap way of sealing and preserving the diaries against damage from the sea air, until Colón could get around to inventing the Tupperware box.

ANOTHER WORLD EXCLUSIVE!!!

Apart from the diaries, which are in themselves a real find, I have also obtained notes and jottings of one of Colón's crew, Able Seaman, Pillager First Class and Freelance Journalist on the '*Genoese Sun*' newspaper, Peg Leg Jake Le Merdok, first mate on the *Santa Maria*. Jake was named 'Peg Leg' at birth, a fact that proved to be strangely prophetic, as for most of his adult life he wore an eye-patch. It is arguably due to Jake's ingenuity[2] that the name Colón is remembered at all.

[2] And light fingers.

YET ANOTHER WORLD EXCLUSIVE !!!

The diaries are lavishly illustrated with many of Colón's original sketches, saved for posterity (i.e. stolen) by Peg Leg Jake. We will see for the first time a number of Colón's navigation charts, which serve to demonstrate his unique (i.e. nonexistent) sense of direction. The diaries also contain a number of sketches of his many inventions. Among these we discover jottings for the first designer trainer, plus his brilliant helicopter blueprint.[3]

AUTHOR'S NOTE [4]

The *Colón Diaries* referred to in this Introduction are newly discovered documents, exclusive to this publication, and should not be confused with the *Columbus Diario*, which up until now has been considered a major source of information about the great explorer.

---

[3] This latter has an interesting story attached to it. The diaries explain how Colón used the back of this blueprint to jot down a recipe for paella, which he then sent to Michelangelo, who was having a dinner party to celebrate his completion of the ceiling of the Sistine Chapel. Unfortunately the dinner party was a washout, as Michelangelo was so exhausted from the years of painting that he fell asleep. The Pope was furious. The paella was delicious.

[4] Not to be confused with a doctor's note, which is completely different.

Well, all I can say is, I've read it and it's rubbish. Now you may consider such a bold statement, coming as it does from someone who is not in fact an historian, is rather outrageous. But consider the facts: the *Columbus Diario* has always been regarded as Colón's own daily log, but it was not published until some twenty-five years after his death, and then only in an edited form. Edited, would you believe it, by a priest called Bartolome De Las Casas. Bartolome De Las Casas? Obviously a made-up name! I mean do you know anyone called anything even remotely resembling such a silly name? I certainly don't. I know someone called Eric Bloaterfish, and I thought that was silly enough, but Bartolome De Las Casas? Ha! Obviously someone down on his luck who decided to cash in on the Colón name. Even the title, *Diario*, sounds like a line from a bad folk song:

> And when he'd discovered Americ-a,
> He wrote it in his Diari-o,
> Diari-o, Diari-o,
> And when he'd discovered Americ-a,
> He wrote it in his Diari-o

9

What is more, 'Brother' De Las Casas makes absolutely no mention of Colón's conker collection, obsession with juggling, colour-blindness, fear of water or any of the other things constantly referred to in the genuine diaries. The other big clincher, of course, is the fact that Brother De Las Casas didn't even get Cristóbal Colón's name right! Proof positive that the *Columbus Diario* is a forgery. But don't just take my word for it – I showed a copy of the *Columbus Diario* to an impartial judge (a girl in our local chip shop) and she was totally unimpressed, so there!

The Fifteenth-Century World

Before we get on to Cristóbal himself, we should consider the general state of the world during this period. These were war-like times. At the start of the century Owen Glendower was leading a Welsh Army against England's Henry IV (parts I and II) in order to obtain independence for Wales. (He failed, of course, and as a direct result some poor people are still forced to take their holidays in Rhyl.)

The Turkish Ottoman Empire (so named because they kept their blankets in small wooden chests) were rampaging through Asia and Europe, virtually destroying the Byzantine Empire (they had a tallboy to look after their blankets), and seriously affecting the trade routes between Spain and the East.

In France the Hundred Years' War was reaching one of its high points, the Battle of Agincourt. The battle took place on Saint Crispin's Day, which gave

William Shakespeare the opportunity to write his famous Saint Crispin's Day speech[5] in his play *Henry V*, which features (not surprisingly) King Henry V, with a very silly haircut, addressing his troops with lots of stuff about 'This day is called Saint Crispin's Day' (for those who didn't know). Imagine if the battle had taken place on an ordinary Thursday! Henry would have been really stuck for a theme for his speech: 'This Day is called . . . er . . . Thursday.' No. It doesn't have the same impact somehow, does it?

The Hundred Years' War eventually came to an end after 93 years (hence the name) when the British burned Joan of Arc at the stake. A small price to pay for peace, although I doubt if Joan saw it that way!

These were indeed dramatic times. Over much of the known world the Christians were fighting the Infidels.[6] The Infidels were basically anyone who wasn't Christian.

'America', as it eventually became known, wasn't at war with anybody. In fact, no-one even knew it was there (except the 'Americans', of course)!

---

[5] Saint Crispin was in fact (and probably still is) the patron saint of Cobblers. Now, had Shakespeare been aware of this he could have peppered King Henry's speech with some fine Elizabethan cobbler jokes, thus making his play marginally less boring than it is. Although, on second thoughts, a quick look at any of Shakespeare's so-called 'comedies' will be enough to make one realise that gags are not his strong point.

[6] This should not be confused with the Christians and the Lions. That was the line-up for the Roman *Superbowl* about 14 centuries earlier.

Putting it on the Map

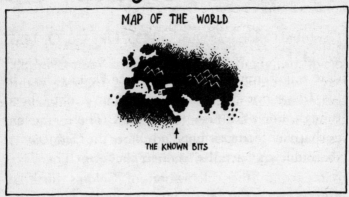

MAP OF THE WORLD

↑
THE KNOWN BITS

Which brings us to another point. In the fifteenth-century the known world was much smaller than it is today. By that I don't mean that bits of the world didn't exist, but that they hadn't yet been discovered. The known world at that time basically consisted of the areas now known as Europe, Africa and Asia (known in those days as the Indies).

This of course had its good side, in that you didn't have to go far to trade with people. Or fight them for that matter. And, since life consisted of a mixture of these two pastimes, things were fine. The down side was the fact that, after all this trading and fighting, everyone needed a well-earned break. But where could you go? There was a very limited choice of holiday venues. No surfing fortnights in Australia, for instance. In fact, no Australia. No sun-soaked luxury cruises to Jamaica. In fact, no Jamaica. But then, the plus side was that, with no Jamaica and no Australia, the English never got beaten at cricket.

The Genoese Connection

Cristóbal Colón was born in 1435. Or 1436. Or 1437. Or 1451. Or five to three or thereabouts. The exact date is not known. Even Bartolome De Las Casas in his *Diario* doesn't trouble to invent a date, even though he invents so much else. There is even, perhaps more surprisingly, no clue in the *Colón Diaries*, thorough and detailed though they are. There is a reference to the celebration of Colón's birthday during his voyage to the New World. Quite a party, by all accounts. Well, by the only existing account, anyway. For the first time in months the crew tasted fresh meat[7], and there was apparently a splendid cake:

> *'A pretty thing it was too, being baked of sixteen fresh goose eggs, and a gross of sultanas.'*

There is also mention of a party, at which the magician was keel-hauled for *'gross sourcery.'* Apparently he did a simple trick and got it right! Oh, why can't you get magicians like that for parties these days? The festivities ended with Colón juggling and challenging everyone in sight to a conker match. Anyone who beat him was thrown over the side. Perhaps that suggests that he was a poor loser but, fair's fair, it was *his* birthday party!

---

[7] It was the ship's cat, actually, but it's amazing what people will eat when they're in a party mood – twiglets, for istance!

So we don't know the date of his birth, though we do know the place – Genoa, a large sea port in Italy. Naturally there have been numerous claims from other countries that Colón was a native of their land, but this often happens in the case of a famous person, and really has more to do with off-loading whole warehouses full of T-shirts, mugs, nodding dogs and other such memorabilia than it has to do with getting at the truth. But it might be worth considering the weight of evidence for and against some of the leading contenders for Cristóbal Colón's birthplace.

GENOA

For: Colón himself (in his diary):

'*I was born in Genoa*'

Against: Dibber the Uncouth (Genoese high street trader [failed]):

'*No he wasn't!*'

Dibber the Uncouth had never been quick to seize a business opportunity. He sunk his entire fortune into little wind-up Christopher Columbus dolls[8] the very week that Colón was brought home from the New World in chains and disgrace. How's that for bad timing! But if Colón's word that Genoa was his birthplace is not enough, let us consider the alternatives:

---

[8] You wound them up and they were seasick. 'Wind 'Em Up and Watch 'Em Chuck!' was the snappy advertising slogan. Cute, eh? They were a disaster. Pity because, although this would come as no consolation to Dibber, they were a very good likeness.

ALICE SPRINGS (AUSTRALIA)

According to the eminent Australian historian and wallaby farmer Ozzie 'Dingo-Breath' Plumstead, Chris Clumbos (as Ozzie insists on calling him) was the son of a poor crocodile-skinner from Alice Springs, who moved to Spain to seek his fortune. This is possible. Colón certainly came from humble stock. But Ozzie's argument has one small flaw. Australia hadn't been discovered in 1435. Or 1436. Or whenever it was that Colón was actually born.

MILTON KEYNES

Frankly a non-starter, but the rumour that Colón was born in or near Milton Keynes won't go away, any more than Milton Keynes itself will, unfortunately. Of course Milton Keynes is only 30 years old. Originally it was the village of Crabs Bottom, but Milton Keynes sounds more majestic, apparently. The rumour was believed to have been started by a minor council official (Edith Scrote, traffic warden of this parish) in the hope of getting Milton twinned with Genoa and earning a cheap holiday.

FRANCE

Yes! Even the French have got in on the act. According to some eminent French person, Colón was in fact born in France and called Culottes. They even named a form of skirt after him. A baggy skirt, attached between the legs giving it the appearance of mediaeval sailors' trousers. But apart from this tenuous link, there is no solid evidence that he was ever born there. Not even once.

PORTUGAL

Not unreasonably there are claims that Colón hailed from Portugal. The one fact that makes this unlikely is that Colón spoke Spanish. However, he also spoke Latin, and Portuguese claimants argue that anyone who could speak Latin could easily have taught himself Spanish, and that he was in fact Portuguese, but chose to speak Spanish all the time. The question this brings to my mind is: why? What possible reason would any self-respecting Portuguese person have for pretending to be Spanish? To impress the girls? Frighten the bank manager? Get an Old Person's One-Day Travel Permit? What? No! It simply makes no sense! Although, as we will see as this book progresses, many of Colón's actions make no sense. But speaking Spanish when you are in fact Portuguese is taking things a bit far, even for Colón!

ITALY

The Italians have never made a big fuss about Cristóbal Colón being Italian. This is probably because they believe that the facts speak for themselves. And the facts are:

1 Cristóbal Colón was born in Genoa
2 Genoa is in Italy.

It is probably reasonable to assume, therefore, that Cristóbal Colón was Italian, which just leaves the confusion about him speaking Spanish.

OTHER PLACES

Well, of course, these are legion. In fact there is barely a village on the planet that hasn't claimed that he was born there, lived there for a bit, slept there on his way to somewhere else, or possibly just stopped there to ask directions. If even half of the claims were true, Colón would never have found time to discover America.

But he *did* find time, and he *did* discover America (more or less).

But more of that later . . . Let us first consider his childhood.

Colons and semi-Colons

So Cristóbal Colón was born in Genoa, Italy, in or around 1435. His father, Domenico, was a wool weaver and trader.

His mother, Susanna, was a woman. As far as we know. Sorry I can't be absolutely certain, but virtually nothing is known about her except her name, Susanna, which is usually a girl's name, even in Italy. And she did come from Italy, from a small mountain village, the inhabitants of which were referred to by outsiders and enemies as 'chestnut eaters', probably because they ate chestnuts. Cristóbal obviously inherited his passion for conkers from his mother's side of the family. But that's all we know about her. You see, in those days it was much more a man's world, than it is now. A woman stayed at home and raised the family. And what a family! There were five children. Four boys: Cristóbal, Bartholomew, Giovanni and Giacomo, and one girl – Bianchinetta.

THE COLON FAMILY

Life wasn't easy for a young man like Domenico, especially with five young mouths to feed. And especially with a name like Colón! Then there was the fact that most cities were run by different families or groups of families, who were constantly fighting. A bit like Mafia families, I imagine. And if you weren't in with the top family, you were right out of it. But in this respect Domenico was lucky. He was able to get on friendly terms with the then ruling family, the Fregosos. Obviously he had done Pietro Fregoso a favour – knitted his wife a nice cardigan or something – and he was rewarded by being made the Keeper of the Olivella Gate.

As you probably know, cities in those days were surrounded by walls to keep strangers out. The walls had gates to let the strangers in. Anyway, one of the gates in Genoa was called the Olivella Gate, and Domenico Colón was the Keeper of it. What exactly this entailed history does not tell us, but one can assume that it involved a certain amount of standing at the gate and challenging strangers as they approached. The dialogue would go something like:

GATE KEEPER: (*In Italian*) Halt! Who goes there? Friend or foe!
STRANGER: (*In Italian*) Friend.
GATE KEEPER: (*In Italian*) Pass, Friend!

Simple! A piece of cake. Money for old rope, really. Assuming that Domenico got paid. Not much point doing the job if he didn't, although I suppose there's a certain amount of kudos attached to it. Great conversation piece:

> 'What do you do for a living?'
> 'Well, as it happens, I'm the Keeper of the Olivella Gate.'
> 'Oh, really?'
> (*Conversation dies.*)

Maybe it's not such a great conversation piece, after all! But it's hardly tasking work. Or is it? Suppose the stranger isn't a friend? What do you do then, eh? Imagine the situation. You're standing at your gate, wearing your special badge or hat, or whatever you get with the job[9], and a stranger approaches:

> YOU: (*In Italian**) Halt! Who goes there? Friend or foe?
> STRANGER: (*In Italian*) Foe.
> YOU: (*In Italian**) Foe?
> STRANGER: (*In Italian*) Yes. Foe.
> YOU: (*In Italian**) Oh. Er. Hang on a minute.
> (* Can we assume for the sake of argument that you speak fluent Italian? Thank you!)

---

[9] I assume you *do* get to wear a special badge or something. Not a lot of point doing the job unless you can dress up a bit, is there?

What do you do? Here you are, Keeper of the Gate, charged with the specific task of keeping out foes, and there's one standing right in front of you. Now, fortunately for you, since yours is a sort of civic appointment, there's bound to be a Gate Keeper's Handbook. You refer to it and discover that you actually don't have the authority to deal with a foe without contacting your superior.

Of course, if this was the twentieth century, you'd give the stranger a withering look, tell him to hang on, and phone your boss. But this is the fifteenth century. Alexander Graham Bell hasn't been born, let alone invented the telephone. So you would have to get a local urchin to run an errand for you, which would cost you, assuming you could find an urchin capable of delivering a message. But let's say that everything goes well, you find your urchin and get him to do the job, and he returns with the message. What will the message say? Well, these are very hard times, remember. So the message probably says: 'Kill the foe.' Now, assuming that the urchin returns with the message written down, you're all right. If he doesn't, then:

YOU: (*In Italian*) Well?
URCHIN: (*Ditto*) Yer Boss says to kill him.
STRANGER: (*In Italian*) Oh. (*Runs Away*)

Of course, if the message is written, then surprise is on your side, but carrying out the instruction is still tricky. Suppose you elect to shoot the foe? This would

involve loading your arquebus (a huge early form of musket) with powder and shot, then placing it on a rest, then aiming it at your victim, then pulling the trigger, which would undoubtedly cause you to fall over from the power of the kick-back. Whether it would cause the victim to fall over from the power of the shot is another matter, because these things were notoriously inaccurate. And, what is more, you have got to achieve all this without your victim realizing what's going on.

The same goes for stabbing:

YOU: (*In Italian, crumpling the note*) Er . . . could you just hang on there a minute while I get a big sharp knife?

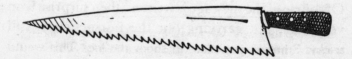

No. It wasn't easy being a Gate Keeper. Certainly it was a task that would have strained the simple mind of a wool trader like Domenico Colón to its limits. And it might have been for this reason that he only lasted in the job for four years. It might have been for this reason, but it wasn't. The reason he didn't retire from the job with a carriage clock and a fat pension was that Pietro Fregoso lost control of the city in a fifteenth century version of the Saint Valentine's Day Massacre.

After that, things went badly for Domenico. He had been known as a supporter of Fregoso, and was out of favour. His business went from bad to worse. Even having a sale every other week didn't help. Mind you, I would have thought that big woollies had a limited appeal in a hot country like Italy. He'd have been better off selling T-shirts or Bermuda shorts[10], but then it's very easy for us to be wise, five hundred or so years after the event, isn't it?

So this was the background to Cristóbal's childhood. A background he was determined to escape from.

A background that he was eventually to deny.

---

[10] Of course they wouldn't have been called Bermuda shorts in those days, because Bermuda hadn't been discovered.

The Happiest Days of Your Life!

To escape the constrictions of humble beginnings a young lad needed an education, preferably a university one. And, in the so-called *Columbus Diario*, Cristóbal Colón is quoted as saying:

'I went to Pavia University'

Alas, this is more wishful thinking than fact. Search as long and hard as you like, you will find no evidence to support his claim. No initials carved in a Pavian tree; no high-jump cup or Latin prize bearing his name; not even a flicker of rememberance from an old caretaker, and everyone knows caretakers live for ever and remember everything. But not even Eduardo Spagbolli, the gnarled old hunchback caretaker of Pavia University, can recall the Discoverer of America. And I do think that, if he'd ever gone there, Spagbolli would have remembered confiscating his ball or catching him smoking, don't you?

So what sort of education did he have? A very modest one, I can reveal. He attended the local elementary school, run by the Clothiers Guild

(Presidents: Signores Marcos and Spencerini), set up to educate the children of wool traders and the like. His was a basic, all-round education, as this school report will show:

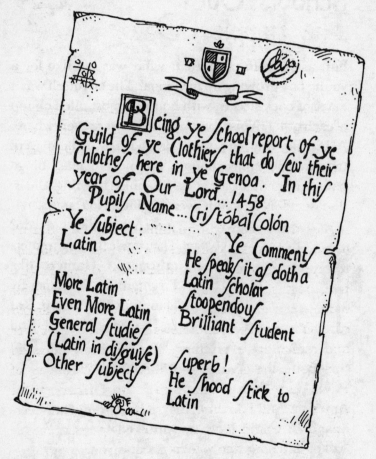

Being ye school report of ye Guild of ye Clothiers that do sew their Chlothes here in ye Genoa. In this year of Our Lord...1458

Pupils Name... Cristóbal Colón

Ye subject:	Ye Comments
Latin	He speaks it as doth a Latin scholar
More Latin	stoopendous
Even More Latin	Brilliant student
General studies (Latin in disguise)	Superb!
Other subjects	He shood stick to Latin

As you can see, Latin was pretty much his strongest subject. Pity he didn't go into the Church, really, then he would have had a use for it!

School's Out!

But, aside from education, what was life like for a young boy growing up in Genoa? The city itself was a maze of back streets, with houses almost piled on top of each other. Noise, bustle and filth were everywhere. A bit like any city these days, really. There were taverns and coffee houses, but no cinemas, bingo halls, amusement arcades, ice-rinks, bowling alleys, discos, etc. No TV, not even satellite. No GAME-BOY!

So what did kids do? They made their own entertainment. Games like Frighten The Pensioner By Dangling The Plague Rat In Her Face On The End Of a Piece of String. That was a popular one.[11]

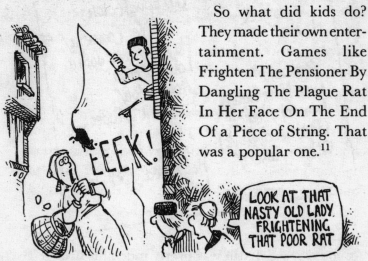

EEEK!

LOOK AT THAT NASTY OLD LADY FRIGHTENING THAT POOR RAT

---

[11] It still would be today, but you just can't get the rats.

Then there was Burning the Heretic.
That was *very* popular. Simple to
set up, but it provided hours of
harmless fun. All you needed
was a large wooden stake,
a Heretic, some good dry
firewood and a box of
matches. Having got
these together you stuck
the stake in the ground,
tied the Heretic to it,
arranged the nice
dry firewood around
the feet of the
Heretic, and then
set fire to it with
the matches. To give
the whole thing a touch of Theatre, not to say
respectability, you could employ the services of a
clergyman. He could be relied on to shout at the
Heretic, telling him how naughty he'd been and how
he would burn in Hell, like as not[12]. The right
combination of really dry firewood and a good
Heretic[13] could pull an enormous crowd. And of
course a clergyman with plenty of rhetoric could
really make the event go with a swing.

---

[12] Which was a stupid thing to say, because the Heretic was
already burning in the High Street.
[13] One who is really, really *not* into the idea of being burned at the
stake.

29

Docklands Development

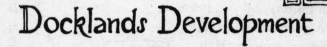

But the real centre of activity, however, in Genoa at least, was the docks. Genoa was a major port, and therefore the docks were a-bustle with traders trying to make money, and pick-pockets trying to relieve them of it. Really the pick-pockets were providing a public service, since many of the tradesmen would only have squandered their earnings in the inns and taverns on the quayside. This way their pockets stayed lighter and their livers intact.

Young Colón would have been drawn to the docks. Not because he was a pick-pocket, although he might have been. Not even because he was a would-be sailor, although he would eventually become one. But because he was interested in commerce, i.e. trading, i.e. making money.

What a place the docks must have been! A thriving, bustling gaggle of people, buying, selling, shouting, singing, laughing. The calls of the traders rent the hot Genoese air:

'Fine spice! Fine spice!'
'Wool! Wool!'
'Dog biscuits! Dog biscuits!'

O.K. Maybe not dog biscuits, but you get the idea! And the ships! All sizes. All shapes. At least all shapes as long as they had a point at the front and were aerodynamic. But what a thrill to meet sailors from countries you could only dream of visiting! What a thrill to hear them speak of the sights they had seen – sights you could not imagine even in your wildest dreams! The young Colón must have spent many hours sitting on an up-turned keg of rum, listening spellbound to the tales of these foreigners, and wondering what the heck they were talking about! Because, remember, Cristóbal spoke only Italian (and Latin), and the visitors probably spoke anything but. But this didn't deter him.

His course was set.

He would go to sea, not as a sailor, but as a merchant. There was more money in it!

Splice The Mainbrace & Pass The Bucket

Young Colón first went to sea at about the age of fourteen. It's hard to say exactly how old he was because we don't know precisely when he was born. However, in his diaries he says:

'I went to sea at Fourteen'

And he should know, even if he couldn't spell 'sea'. And, yes, O.K., so he also thought America was India, but he might be able to get a simple thing like his own age right, mightn't he? Oh, well, to be on the safe side let's say he first went to sea as a teenager, but not as a sailor. Most of his early journeys would have been made on his father's business. In the days that his father still had a business, that is. He would have stood on the deck of the ship, watching the sailors splicing the mainbrace, letting go for'ard and so on, and wondering what on earth they were doing. Because as I have already pointed out our Cris was not a natural sailor. Nevertheless, as he stood there on the prowp or poo deck or whatever it was called, he had that unmistakeable glint in his eye. A glint only an Old Salt can interpret immediately. A glint that usually means that the 'glinter' is about to throw up!

Ah, seasickness! The curse of nautical men everywhere. And nautical women probably, although women generally tend to have stronger stomachs. But many a fine sailor has suffered from it. Forget scurvy, Capstan Blight and Moby Dick – seasickness has carried off more old seadogs than all of them put together. Even Admiral Lord Nelson, he of Trafalgar and Lady Hamilton fame, suffered greatly from it. It's a little-known fact that his famous message to the fleet during the Battle of Trafalgar has never been reported in full. Not until this moment. In fact, the full message read: 'England Expects Every Man To Do His Duty . . . Ooops! Excuse me!'

Over the years there have been a multitude of seasickness remedies, none of which really worked, of course. And in the mid-fifteenth century things were no different. But that didn't prevent self-styled chemists from trying to solve the problem. I have obtained the following document, printed by an early printing method – a complex combination of potato cuts and string:

'Ye Cur for Ye See-Sickness upon high Seez[14]
1. Being ye first cure:
Take ye a posset of Cider. Add to this a bushel of warm Badgerz blood, a gram of nutmeg. ye leg off a bee caught on ye wing. Drink ye swift as ye chant allowed, 'Oh Lord take this sickness from my stomick!'

---

[14] And that's what they charged for it – high fees!

Now, you wouldn't need to be any kind of a genius to spot the basic flaw in this particular cure. Namely, how are you going to 'chant allowed' (I imagine they mean 'aloud') anything, let alone 'Oh, Lord! take thi*f* . . . etc.' while drinking? Even a fully trained ventriloquist can only do the alphabet, and even then it comes out as 'Aye, Gee, Cee, Gee, Eee, Heff, Gee . . . etc.' So a seafaring person who is feeling decidedly 'dicky' has got no chance. But there is another, more obvious, flaw in this cure. Warm badger's blood? The leg of a bee caught on the wing? Where are you going to get those in the middle of an ocean? The answer is, you aren't. Unless of course you send someone to find the ingredients:

You can easily see how mutinies started, can't you? Fortunately sailors now have a Seamen's Union to negotiate proper rates for going to fetch the leg of a bee caught on the wing, etc., but in those days they could be exploited mercilessly.

Anyway, there stood our hero, Cristóbal Colón, on the deck of the ship, feeling sick, but he was at home. Well, he wasn't at home, he was at sea, but such was his appalling sense of direction that he *thought* he was at home. Or, at least, he *felt* that he was at home.

But these little trading trips were to be his greatest adventures for a few years more. His Greatest Adventure of all, across the Atlantic Ocean, was still a long way off.

An Explorer in Waiting

Life for Colón in his late teens and early twenties was far from uneventful. Although much of this time was spent trading for his father, he did branch out on his own, and in 1474 he went to live on the island of Chios, just off Turkey, and traded in gum. What a step forward! From trading in wool to trading in gum! Boy, did he know how to live! However, it was during this period that he first displayed any talent for invention.

The *Colón Diaries* take up the story:

'One day, on Chios, I was up a gum tree. Then jumped I too the grownde, holding my robes tite arownde mee for modestie. Thus saw I not the poodle of mastik gum, there dripped on the grownde by the tree.'

The upshot was that the mastic stuck to his shoes, forming a thick crêpe sole, which he found impossible to remove. The only thing he could do was cut the mastic to the shape of his sole and put up with it. However, he soon realized that the rubber sole provided an excellent grip, and he began to consider the possibilities of making a simple shoe from sail canvas, then coating the bottom with mastic. After a few false starts (see illustrations) he eventually achieved his aim. He called his invention *Tre-Hon-Aere*, which loosely translated means 'shoe with a sticky bottom'.

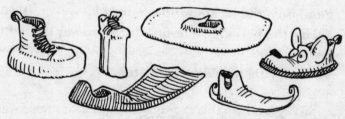

Unfortunately, as with most of Colón's ideas, no-one could quite see the point of these shoes. In fact it wasn't until he met a group of monks from the monastery of San Lucia de La Ministroni that his invention was put to good use. The monks belonged to the Holy Order of the Bowl, and had been traditional brothmakers to the Crusaders for many centuries – a sort of Holy Army Catering Corps. The problem had always been getting the Great Tureen, a massive seven-gallon broth bowl, to the soldiers across slippery wet rocks and suchlike without falling over and spilling it. The monastery issue rope sandals provided

no grip at all. It was a real problem. Until Cristóbal came along. He was able to kit the entire monastery out in his new *Tre-Hon-Aeres*, which the monks quickly renamed in Latin *Supo-Maftix*, or 'Broth-Crêpes'. Folk legend suggests that Colón refused payment for his good deed, but the monks were now beholden to him, and doubtless he would find a way for them to repay him eventually.

But apart from this exciting interlude, our hero was drifting. Well, not drifting exactly. Sailing under canvas. Although that is a form of drifting, I suppose. But I was referring really to the purpose of his life. It didn't have one. True, he was gaining trading and sailing experience. He had now thrown up in every known ocean. He had, for instance, sailed to England. Or at least he would have done, but for the fact that his ship was attacked by French pirates, and sunk. Cristóbal survived by swimming ashore.

'I'm just popping ashore for some warm badger's blood,' he told his crew mates as he jumped over the side.

He went to Ireland, but couldn't speak the language any better than most of the locals could. Also it was cold. He did eventually reach England after that earlier false start, and settled for a while in Bristol. That was cold too. What the Bristol locals made of him is not known, although I imagine that they were rather amazed, as he insisted on talking to them in Latin. What a show-off! They probably just assumed that he was a lunatic and left him alone. That's how people in Bristol usually treat strangers. In my experience, anyway.

From Bristol he sailed to Iceland. It was even colder. Little is known about these trips, other than the fact that they were trading trips. And cold.

Oh! There is one rivetting piece of information that comes out of this period! The Icelandic people were apparently very impressed by his grey eyes! How we should know this, or why anyone would bother to report it, I cannot tell.

However, it does lead us to one of the other great mysteries about the soon-to-be Discoverer of America: what did he look like? Perhaps this might be as good a time as any to sift through the available evidence and try to put together our own Identikit picture of Cristóbal Colón . . .

Do You Know this Man?

It is difficult to get an exact picture of Cristóbal Colón. Those pictures of him that do exist are not very accurate, as he never sat for a portrait. But we can get a reasonable idea of his appearance from other writings. So, what do we know about him:

1 He was apparently taller than average. What does that mean? You probably know that the height of your average human has increased over the years. You have only to visit an Elizabethan house to realize the truth of that. Shakespeare must have been short, judging from his house. The ceilings are so low there that unless he was short, he would have been banging

his head continually. (Mind you, that might explain the plots of some of his plays.) Colón was born at least a hundred years earlier than the Bard of Stratford, and so it's fair to assume that he was even shorter. But, even though he might only have been about five foot tall, he was probably a bit of a hunk by fifteenth-century standards.

2 He had red hair. Yes, apparently this is true. A number of independent sources have confirmed this. In fact, in the *Colón Diaries* he remarks on the irritation of having his crew members call out 'Whotcha, Ginger!' It took a long time for him to realize that they were referring to him, on account of his colour-blindness. It is also known that he went grey at an early age. About thirty, in fact, which in those days wasn't an early age at all, when you consider that living to fifty was bit of a novelty. This was largely due to the lack of medical knowledge. They didn't have the hospitals we have these days. Mind you, they didn't have the waiting lists either. In those days you could catch a disease, have no idea what it was, and die from it all in the space of an afternoon. Anyway, Cristóbal Colón had red (grey) hair.

RED   GREY   GREEN   CHESTNUT

3 He had grey eyes. At least he did according to the people of Iceland. Why we should know this I really don't understand, but apparently it is an accepted fact. Possibly he visited Iceland several times, and the headline in the local newspaper, the *Iceland and Fish Fancier's Times*, read: 'Old Grey-Eyes Is Back!'. He also had a piercing stare, according to some reliable source. It was probably a confused glare, actually.

PIERCING STARE

PIERCING STAIRS

Bear in mind he was an Italian merchant who spoke Italian and Latin, trying to trade with Englishmen, Irishmen and Icelanders, and wondering why they didn't instantly understand him. Still, he had grey eyes. Although they might have been blue.

So, if you'd been around in the late fifteenth century and you'd seen a tall/short bloke with grey/blue eyes and red/grey hair, it was probably Cristóbal Colón – or somebody else.

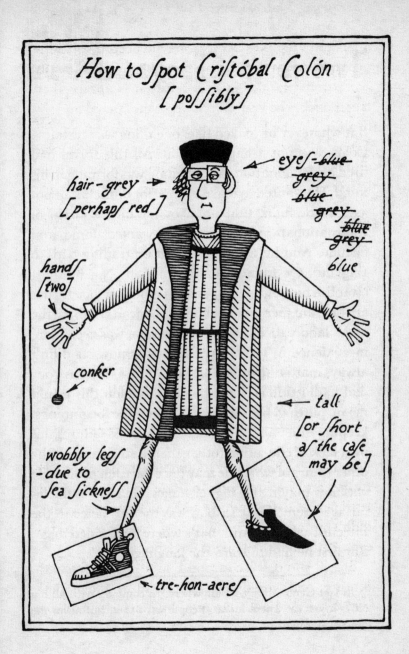

Time for a Change

But whatever he looked like, one thing was certain –
Colón was not a happy person. All this travel had
fired his imagination. An ambition was forming in his
mind. He wanted to make a name for himself. But not
as a tradesman. Oh, no! Not for him a chain of
International Superstores! He wanted fame and
fortune. And he wouldn't find it on trading trips to
England. Or Ireland for that matter. No, he must
establish himself as a respected member of society, not
an itinerant merchant. This would mean climbing the
social ladder, because the class system was even more
in evidence in those days than it is now. It didn't
always matter how capable you were, as long as your
dad had a title or some land. For Colón this would
mean putting behind him his humble beginnings,
keeping quiet about his father's business failures, his
own lack of education (other than Latin), and all the
other things of which he may once have felt proud. He
was now playing for higher stakes. Genoa was fine as
far as it went[15], but Lisbon was the 'in' place in the
fifteenth century. And that's where he decided to go.
But first he had to learn the language.

---

[15] In fact Genoa didn't go anywhere. In common with all big
cities it just sat where it was. People went to it, but never the
other way round.

Back to School

These days, if you want to learn a new skill, but you've left school (or it isn't on the syllabus), you can just pop along to your local education offices and enrol for a course somewhere. This is true of almost anything from train-spotting to microsurgery. Why, these days you can even get a GCSE in tourism! But not so in fifteenth-century Italy. Some of the schools were just a bench in some rich person's back garden. So anything extra-curricular was right out! Your only chance of learning, say, another language, was to find someone to teach you privately. This usually meant a monk or some other churchman.

Monks in those days were a clever lot (still are). Apart from having more than a working knowledge of Latin, they knew Greek, had read most of the classics, could sing, dance, make brilliant jam – in fact there was hardly anything worth knowing that monks didn't know. They even knew things that weren't worth knowing. So naturally it was to a monk that Colón took himself. After all, being a devout Catholic, he knew his fair share of religious men with funny haircuts, including Father Thomas[16]. Although basket-work and macramé were Thomas's particular passions[17], he was no slouch when it came to foreign languages.

Father Thomas was a good teacher. Cristóbal was a quick learner. He grabbed the language by the vowels. He threw himself into it, as he did with most things. Like the sea. And he conquered the language, as he would conquer the sea some years later. In what seemed like minutes, but was in fact months, he had mastered the entire language from *No comprendo* (I do not understand) to *Habla Usted Latin?* (Do you speak Latin?) In fact he learned to speak it like a native, so much so that many people thought he *was* a native. Oh, yes! Cristóbal Colón, late of Genoa but soon to live in Lisbon, could now speak perfect Spanish – no problem!

Although, of course, there was a problem. And the problem was: Lisbon was in Portugal![18]

---

[16] The former Luigi Sagopudini, who had taken his religious name from the least self-assured of Christ's disciples. This was mainly due to his basic insecurity about even the simplest matter, and his irritating habit of saying: 'Oöoh, I'm not sure about that!'

[17] Praying was also quite high on his list of likes and dislikes.

[18] In fact Lisbon still is in Portugal.

The Lisbon Years

In his mid-twenties, Cristóbal Colón became convinced that there was another route to the Indies[19]. The current route was through the Straits of Gibraltar, turn left around the bottom of Africa, and ask again (although nobody knew you could do this). Or out through the Straits, turn right past France and Scandinavia, up round the top of what is now Russia, and ask again. Or through the Black Sea and ask again. But these were dangerous routes. Not only were the seas hazardous, but continual fighting with the Turks and Moors (not to mention each other!) meant that many ships were lost.

[19] The Indies in those days were made up of India, China and Japan. They were major exporters of spices and other exotic goods.

Colón argued that the Indies could be reached by going straight on at the Straits across the Atlantic, without having to ask again. He calculated that the Indies were only about 3,000 miles away by following that route. He was wrong, but he didn't let a little thing like that get in his way. In fact, the Indies were 12,000 miles away and America was in the way, but nobody knew that.

Of course, there had been indications that there might be a strange country sitting out in the Atlantic somewhere. Strange plants and bits of trees had been washed up on the shores of Europe. There was even a rumour that a lone helmsman was washed up among bits of a wrecked ship. This lone helmsman apparently spoke only to Cristóbal Colón, telling him of a New World, but all this has been dismissed as idle gossip. After all, if some dying sailor had given Colón a map of America, why did he continue to believe that the Atlantic was empty, and a clear route to the Indies? And not only did Colón believe it, but he spent the next fifteen years trying to convince everybody else. It became his 'dream'.

But first he had to earn a living while he studied navigation and seamanship, on dry land (true). So he went to work for his younger brother Bartholomew in Lisbon, the capital city of Portugal. Bartholomew had a thriving map- and chart-making business. But doubtless he was glad of his brother's help. After all, Cristóbal had travelled fairly extensively and could possibly correct any inaccuracies in the existing maps. Possibly, although it's unlikely that he did.

You see, in those days map-making was not the exact science that it is now. I mean, these days you can buy a map virtually anywhere, open it up, look for Acacia Avenue, go there and find a neat row of mock Tudor-style houses. But in those days a map didn't go into that kind of detail. It was accurate as far as it went, but crude.

However, the sea charts were full of islands. The sailors of the day liked their islands even if they didn't exist, and the more exotic the better. In fact, if you wanted to make any kind of name for yourself in the cut-throat world of map-making, you had to have the best islands:

MAP-SELLER: Good morning, sir. Can I help you?

CUSTOMER: Yeah. I'd like a map.

MAP-SELLER: Certainly, sir. This is our latest model.

CUSTOMER: Huh! That's no good!

MAP-SELLER: Why? What's wrong with it?

CUSTOMER: Well, just look at it! Not many islands on it, are there?

MAP-SELLER: Oh, well . . .

CUSTOMER: I saw one yesterday. It had hundred of islands, it did. All over it! It had one the shape of a star and a little batch of islands just off the Canaries called Wood Pigeon Islands. Why, it even had a couple on dry land! Now, that's what I call a map!

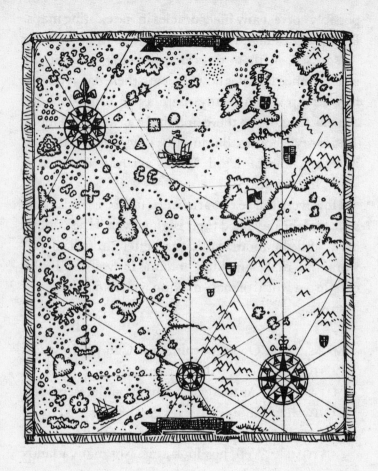

And so, because competition was so fierce, the most successful map-maker was the one with the most highly developed imagination.

But life wasn't all sailing, trading and map-forging for the young hot-blooded future Admiral of the Ocean Sea during these Lisbon years. They were also . . .

The Married Years

Now, at this point I would love to be able to tell you a tale of romance, of star-crossed lovers meeting in secret because their parents didn't approve, of love triumphing against all odds. But it just didn't happen that way. Sorry, but there were no midnight trysts, no climbing towards each other over the heads of a subway station full of commuters like in *Crocodile Dundee*, nothing like that.

Cristóbal Colón met Felipa Perestrello at church, which is presumably where he married her in 1480. We know nothing about what she looked like, but we do know that she was well connected. By that I don't mean that her arms and legs were stuck on properly – I mean her family had friends in high places. And this would have made her very attractive to the ambitious young Colón, who was looking for people to finance the plan to cross the Atlantic even now forming in the brain under his red (or grey) hair.

Whatever Felipa looked like, she caught Cristóbal's grey (or blue) eye, and they were married. And things immediately started to get better. Felipa's brother turned out to be the Governor of Porto Santo, one of the Madeira Islands. (Well, I say 'turned out to be' but you can't tell me that someone as sharp as Cris didn't already know this. After all, he spoke three languages, even if one of them was Latin!) Wasting no time, the newly-weds rushed off to stay with the Governor on Porto Santo. Another stroke of luck was the fact that Felipa's late father had been a great sailor and navigator, and Cristóbal was given access to all his sea charts, log books and maps. And the more he studied them, the more possible his dream seemed to become. But for one thing. He needed cash!

How was he to get it? Certainly he was moving in moneyed circles, even if he didn't have any himself. He was wining and dining with the cream of Porto Santo society, and as the Governor's brother-in-law he was well respected, even if he was an ex-gum salesman. But he could hardly lean over the table during dinner and say, 'You don't fancy slipping me a couple of million so that I can sail across the Atlantic, do you?' That is just the sort of thing you do not do in polite society[20]! No. If he was ever to realize his dream, Colón needed a backer.

It was about this time that Portugal caught Gold Fever.

---

[20] Any more than you'd lean over the dinner table and say: 'Excuse me, but did you know you've got a huge great Green Gilbert dangling out of your left nostril?'

There's Gold in Them There Foreign Parts

In the early 1480s, the Portuguese discovered a large amount of gold on the African coast, in a place now known as Ghana. They called it La Mina (the mine). Although gold had been around for some time, the size of the discovery made many people realize that there must be lots more elsewhere, just waiting to be taken. O.K., so it really belonged to the locals, but they were mostly backward heathens who could never appreciate it.

So a number of 'crusades' were set up. Portuguese soldiers would arrive in a foreign land, relieve the locals of their tiresome gold and teach them about God. This was called conversion. They converted the locals from being a greedy, money-grabbing heathen race into a penniless, God-fearing one. Not that God had any say in the matter! The gold was then used to finance Holy Wars- the term used to describe a war where the Good Guys (the Portuguese) fought the Bad Guys (everyone else) and relieved them of their lands, money, and any spare gold they might have had lying around.

Colón himself got involved. He was able, through his wife's family connections and despite the fact that he spoke fluent Spanish, to get a passage on a Portuguese ship to Guinea. This really opened his eyes. For one thing it served to dispel a few sailors' myths. The ship didn't burst into flames as it sailed near the Equator, as he had been told it would. Neither did his head turn back-to-front. (Mind you, no-one had ever suggested that it would, so that didn't surprise him in the slightest.) The trip gave Colón a real taste for adventure. It also gave him a taste for gold. And, if he could only find that elusive Western trade route to the Indies, who knows what other treasures might be heaped on his head? It was time to realize his Dream.

Goodbye, Mrs Colón

Unfortunately, around this time, Cristóbal's wife died. They had one son, Diego. Colón was now a one-parent family – just him and his little boy. Imagine them together in front of a roaring fire, Colón telling little Diego bedtime stories or teaching him the finer points of conkers, the little hints: soaking them in vinegar, sticking them in the oven for a while to harden them up. (Does that make them more brittle or tougher? Colón would have known.) Perhaps, late at night, he stroked his sleeping son's hair and whispered of his great dream, the Western Passage.

But I don't think so, somehow. Cristóbal Colón was too obsessed with his dream to worry about his son. So what happened to him? Did his dad put him in a day-care centre? Put his name down for the local playschool? Send him to boarding school? Who knows? It's possible that he was looked after by monks or his grandma, Cristóbal's mother-in-law. Yes, that's far more likely.

I'm glad we've got that sorted out. It would have been a load off Colón's mind as he prepared for the big event. Big event? Oh, yes! Didn't I tell you? Through his contacts at the Portuguese court, Colón had obtained an interview with King John II, the newly crowned King of Portugal.

It was 1484. Cristóbal Colón was thirty-three(ish) and very sure of himself. The king couldn't refuse.

A Word in Your Ear, Your Majesty

So Colón's Big Chance had arrived – the chance to ask the King of Portugal for the money to finance a voyage across the Atlantic Ocean to discover the Western route to the Indies. Remember, there was no thought in his mind of discovering anything as big as America. Oh, naturally, he thought he might find a few islands on the way, but that's all. As far as he and everyone else was concerned, there was no large landmass in the Atlantic. If only they'd known!

What's more, Colón had to play his sales pitch just right. He wouldn't get a second chance. After all, he was dealing with royalty. And when royalty says no, they mean no. That was as true in the fifteenth century as it is today. The only difference is that in the fifteenth century they would very likely chop your head off for good measure, just in case you were thinking of arguing about it. So, Cris would have his work cut out. He had to present his case to the very best of his ability. But how?

Of course, if it happened today, he'd call in the

experts – some firm with a name like Stedgeway, Hampton, Truss, Wippett and Throb. A marketing company would write a fancy speech for him and produce a glossy brochure and some slides. They might even make a video! Yes! Get some top-flight actors and an award-winning director and make a short film of the voyage. Get John Williams (*Star Wars*, etc.) or Andrew Lloyd Webber (everything else) to write the music.

But none of these things existed then. He would have to rely on his powers of oratory. And his working model. Yes! According to The *Colón Diaries* he did take along a little model of the Earth, made from an orange with the various countries painted on it. He had used it in his efforts to calculate the exact width of the Ocean. Unfortunately, he made the mistake of using a satsuma instead of a Jaffa, which put his calculations out by 9,000 miles, but no-one could possibly have known that at the time!

So what was he asking for? Simple. Cash. Enough cash to provide ships, crews and provisions for a journey to the East Indies, travelling in the wrong direction. Now, in order to understand the way Colón's mind was working you had to accept that the world was round, and in the fifteenth century most intelligent people believed it was. Not everyone did, obviously.

Many people were still convinced that it was flat. Some believed it was like a dish being carried on the backs of four elephants,  who were standing on the shell of a turtle. A turtle! That's some circus trick, eh? Four elephants on the shell of a turtle! I mean, I know elephants are clever[21], but that's ridiculous! And then there have always

been the nutters who believe that the world is square, pear-shaped, made of Play-Dough or non-biodegradeable lavatory paper, etc., etc.

---

[21] I once saw one step over a woman in a pink gingham dress without crushing her. There was a tense hush from the crowd as the elephant started his walk, followed by a great moan of disappointment when not even a tiny drop of blood was spilled.

Fortunately for Cris most of the Court of the King of Portugal accepted that the world was round, so that wasn't a problem. The problem was this: what exactly was the trip going to achieve? After all, Colón was simply going to sail to somewhere that everyone already knew about, but he was going to take the long way round. What he needed to do was to convince the king that there were lots of islands in the Atlantic that were full of gold and other exciting stuff, and naturally the king would get the biggest share of it all[22]. But how could he do that? He had no evidence to support such claims.

No, he had only one argument to put forward: the journey wasn't very long, and it would give the king a safer route to the Indies.

Picture the scene. Cristóbal Colón, in his best robe, standing behind a fifteenth century version of a fold-away table groaning under the weight of his papers and calculations, star charts and navigation drawings. He probably took along one of his brother's maps with a particularly exotic selection of invented islands drawn on it, just as a clincher. But just how did navigators calculate distances to places in the fifteenth century? I'll tell you:

---

[22] Naturally Cris wanted his cut!

Calculating a Dream

All you needed to know was the exact latitude and longitude of a country, and the exact size of the world. Then you counted the number of longitude lines between the 'you are here' arrow and the place you wanted to reach, multiplied it by the distance between each longitude line, and you got the distance! Simple-pimple! The only ways you could go wrong were:

1 Not knowing the exact position of the place you wanted to reach.
2 Not knowing the exact position of the place you were to start with.
3 Not knowing the exact size of the Earth.
4 Not knowing the exact distance between the longitude lines.
5 Not knowing anything at all, including the names of simple household objects.
6 Being completely mad.

Other than that, it was simple!

Meanwhile, Back at Court

Cristóbal Colón started his pitch. Surrounded by all his paraphernalia, his orange/globe, bits of string, charts, etc., he started to spout. It must have been impressive. It probably went on a bit, because he wasn't the sort of bloke to miss an opportunity to show off. More than likely he would have popped in a few anecdotes, a bit of dinner party chit-chat, name-dropping, etc., just to impress[23]. When at last he finished, there might have been polite applause. There might not have been. How can I possibly be expected to know? I wasn't there, was I?

History tells us that the king did not give Colón an answer there and then. Imagine the embarrassment! The horrible silence while he rolled up all his charts, gathered together his working model of the voyage, and nervously started peeling the orange (realized and stopped before devouring his working model), rolled up the bits of string[24], and carefully packed it all in his bag. He hadn't bargained for this. He honestly thought that the king would jump[25] at the idea. If he'd

---

[23] He shouldn't have bothered. It's impossible to impress royalty. Not only have they seen it all, they've *got* it all!

[24] There *must* have been string. There always is!

[25] Another big mistake. Royalty simply do not jump. They do not hop or skip either.

known this was going to be the reaction, he'd probably have hired a juggler to fill in while he packed his stuff. But he hadn't. So he packed in silence, then went home to wait.

He wasn't overly bothered. After all, this was a chance of a lifetime. The king couldn't possibly turn him down, could he? He just needed time to chew it over. After all, King John II had only been on the throne for five minutes, metaphorically speaking. He'd probably want to talk it over with his advisors.

If Colón thought this, he was right.

The king did discuss it with his advisors. Well, the advisors were bound to give the idea the thumbs up, weren't they?

If Colón thought this, he was wrong. The king, on the advice of his ministers, turned Cris down flat.

Why? Where had he gone wrong? Well, apart from the fact that the Portuguese couldn't really see what was in it for them, they simply didn't like him. They thought he was a big-head. As one of them put it at the time: *"The fellow is a boaster and a bigg tawker,"* which roughly translated means big-head.

All his hard work gone to waste! They didn't want to know! Even the fact that he had miscalculated the distance between Portugal and the Indies via the Atlantic by 9,000 miles by using the wrong size orange didn't matter in the slightest, because the Portuguese just weren't interested. It's tough, but history is full of these little twists of fate. An apple fell on Sir Isaac Newton's head, and because of that he discovered gravity. However, if four tons of falling masonry had fallen on his head he would have discovered his lack of accident insurance.

Ah, well . . . such is fate!

And fate was clearly not on Cristóbal Colón's side.

Back to the Map-Drawing Board

Disappointed, Cristóbal Colón returned to his brother's shop in Lisbon. Did I say disappointed? I meant furious! Yes! He paced Bartholomew's shop floor, cursing. He did it in Latin, just to show off. He accosted any customer who would listen[26] and said things like:

'How could King John II turn me down?'[27]

'Who does he think he is?'[28]

'He doesn't know what he's missing!'[29]

'He'll be sorry!'[30]

'Right! That's it! I won't ask him again!'[31]

Of course much of this was wasted on the average customer, because they didn't speak Spanish. You see, having learned the language, Cris was pig-

---

[26] They didn't have a lot of choice if they ever wanted their maps!

[27] Easily. After all, he was King.

[28] He thought he was King John II of Portugal. It was George III of England who was the loony. He thought he was a bowl of geraniums.

[29] But then neither did anyone else!

[30] Very true. He was. Eventually.

[31] Not true. He did. Or at least, he tried to. But, as you will see later, he was pipped at the post.

headed enough to use it at every available opportunity. But, let's face it, what else could he do? How would he raise the money? Have a jumble sale? Put an ad in the local paper? Ask someone else?

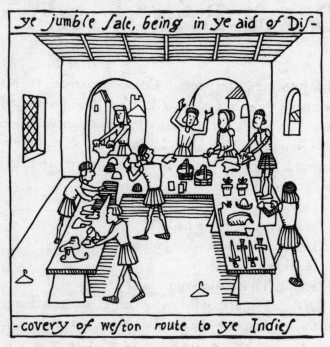

ye jumble Sale, being in ye aid of Dis-covery of weston route to ye Indies

That's it! But who? The Italians were a waste of time. They were too busy fighting each other. The Portuguese had just turned him down. That only left the Spanish. After all, it had to be someone he could talk to. And he spoke Spanish like a native. That was the answer, then. Spain. And so that's exactly what he did. He decided to ask the Spanish monarchs. They were bound to say yes!

Viva España!

At this time Spain was under the rule of Ferdinand and Isabella, who were young and go-ahead. Like Portugal, Spain had caught gold fever. Like Portugal, they had gone around converting people and relieving them of their gold. But, unlike Portugal, they were really, really good at it! So much so they even started their own Spanish Inquisition. Boy! Was that fun, or what? You see, Ferdinand and Isabella were devoutly religious. They were Christian, which in those days basically meant Catholic. Everyone was answerable to the Pope, and the Pope had a hot-line to 'Upstairs'. Ferdinand and Isabella believed that anyone who didn't recognize the Pope as the head of the Church was a heathen. But did they say to themselves, or rather to each other: 'Oh, well! It takes all sorts, doesn't it? Live and let live, that's the way I look at it!'?

Did they heck! Instead, they felt compelled to convert everyone to their faith, or make them die in the attempt. So they went around torturing, burning, and generally reducing the quality of life[32] for anyone they thought of as a 'non-believer'. And Cris was hoping to appeal to their generous nature!

Some hope!

But that's what he did. He moved to Spain, to the port of Palos, where the monks at La Rabida did a very good Bed and Breakfast. He took little Diego with him. The boy was now four. He would try his luck at the court of Ferdinand and Isabella. Learning Spanish was to come in handy after all!

---

[32] i.e. ending it!

The Spanish Archer

Cristóbal Colón used all his influence (or, more accurately, the influence of his dead wife's relatives) to get an audience with the Spanish monarchs. Again he dusted off his charts, logs, orange, bits of string and numerous calculations. Again he put on his best suit. Had a shave, probably. May even have had a wash, although washing wasn't as popular in the fifteenth century as it is these days.

And off he went, still confident, but mindful that he had been rejected once already. Still, this time would be different, wouldn't it? He struggled to convince himself:

'After all, I'm Spanish! Well, my mouth is, anyway! I'm almost a Spanish subject, from neck to nose!'

Yes, O.K., it's not an argument that would convince many people, but he was getting desperate. If only Ferdinand and Isabella had realized that they couldn't turn him down! But they didn't[33], and they did[34]. Flat.

---

[33] Realize.
[34] Turn him down.

At least, Ferdinand turned him down flat. Isabella was a little less heartless[35]. She could see that Cris was sincere. She could also see the holes in his tights. So she gave him some money and servants, and effectively made him part of the Royal Household.

Now, it was suggested at the time that Isabella rather fancied our Cris. After all, he wasn't a bad looking bloke, probably. Short or tall, with red or grey hair and blue or grey eyes, who could resist him? But, for all that he had found favour with Isabella, he had still been turned down. Why? Well, it actually took a select committee of very learned Spaniards a year to decide that it wouldn't work. Their basic argument was this:

1 If it was possible to sail west to reach the Indies, somebody else would have done it already. A Spaniard, probably. A proper Spaniard, not just an Italian who spoke Spanish, but still had ice-cream dribbles on his shirt.[36]

2 Even if it was possible, the voyage would take three years, even for a proper Spaniard, not just . . . etc.[37]

---

[35] That must have really blown her credibility as Head of the Spanish Inquisition!

[36] Not true.

[37] Not true.

3 Even if it was possible and didn't take three years, even for an etc., you would eventually just wind up back at Spain, because the world was round[38].

4 Even if it was possible, didn't take three years, even etc., and you didn't end up back in Spain, you'd never get back. The reason being that the moment you left the western hemisphere, you'd start going downhill, because the world was round, and you'd never find a wind strong enough to blow you back.[39]

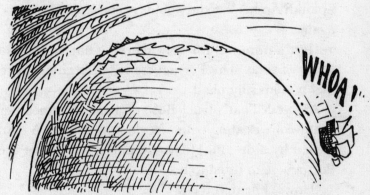

5 Even if it was possible, didn't take three years, even etc., you didn't wind up back in Spain or find that you couldn't get back, they didn't like the look of this Colón bloke anyway and didn't see why they should help him[40].

---

[38] Not true. Well, the bit about the world being round was true, but the rest was rubbish.
[39] Well, you probably realize that that's not true, without me saying it!
[40] Fair enough!

Faced with such weighty intellect, there wasn't much Cris could do but pack up, go home to Genoa, pick up his needles, rejoin the family wool business (if they still had one) and forget all about it.

And that's exactly what he didn't do! Because, remember, he was a Big Head. He thought that they would probably change their minds! And in fact he was proved right, but not yet. He would have to wait.

So, in the meantime, he needed other strings to his bow. Ferdinand and Isabella had given him the Spanish Archer[41], so he would try elsewhere. Portugal again.

'Just a minute!' I hear you cry! 'That's a bit of a waste of time. The Portuguese hate his guts, not to mention his silly plan!'

Ah, yes! That's true! But you have to remember that we are dealing with a devious man here. A man driven by a dream. He would find a way to get the Portuguese to listen to his idea.

'How?' I hear you ask.

'Easy,' I reply. By sending his brother!

---

[41] A slang expression, meaning the push, boot, sack, or dismissal. Believed to relate back to mediaeval times when the legendary Spanish archer, El Bow (also known as The Big E), walked the plains of Spain (where the rain mainly falls), offering his services as a huntsman. Such was his lack of ability with the long bow, or the short bow for that matter, that he rarely lasted more than five minutes in any job, either because he was fired or because he had accidentally shot his new employer.

Having a Terrible Time - Wish You Were Here!

Poor old Bartholomew Colón! Things had been much calmer at the shop while Cris had been away at the Spanish court, bending the Royal Ear. But suddenly his quiet afternoons spent inventing sillier and sillier names for imaginary islands were shattered. He was now a Man With A Mission, or rather the Brother of a Man with a Mission. Cristóbal had bullied him into going to see King John II of Portugal.

'Oh, come on!' I can hear Cris saying. 'The Palace is only round the corner! You can do it in your lunch break!'

Well, however Cristóbal persuaded him, Bartholomew agreed to go and see the king, while his big brother returned to Spain.

Would Bartholomew Colón be successful? We'll never know, because while he was waiting for an audience, another explorer, the famous Bartholomew Diaz[42], returned from a trip in African waters. Maybe he was given Bartholomew Colón's audience with the king by mistake. After all, they had similar names. It's a simple mistake to make.

---

[42] What do you mean, you've never heard of him? He was famous. At least he was in Portugal!

Anyway, it turned out that Diaz pipped Colón to the post. He had gone through the Straits of Gibraltar, turned left around the bottom of Africa and, without even asking again, had discovered the southern route to the Indies. He had even brought back some joss sticks. Well, you can imagine the reaction! No more treacherous Black Sea route for these smart Portuguese cookies! It was the Africa route for them from now on! Seeing the way things were going[43], Bartholomew didn't even wait around long enough for the king to say, 'Cristóbal *who*?'

He packed the charts, string and orange back into his bag, and left. He would have to write to his brother and tell him. He would have to catch him in a good mood. He started looking for a really funny postcard. In fact Cris took it remarkably well. Some lesser people would have sent their brother to Coventry for letting them down, but not him.

He sent Bartholomew to France[44]. Then he sent him to England[45]. He wasn't going to give up!

---

[43] They'd got the cocoa and biscuits out, and were really set to party!
[44] To see King Charles VIII
[45] To see King Henrty VII

A Change of Heart - A Change of Shirt

While Bartholomew was away in Portugal, France and England, being laughed at and generally humiliated on his brother's behalf[46], Cristóbal wasn't sitting about idly, oh, no! He was partying! 'Networking' they call it now. Basically, this means you go to lots of social events, meet people you may need to do business with in the future, and then spend the next few days trying to remember who they were!

[46] Would you do that for your brother? Be honest now!

Cris had no such trouble. He was past master at this 'networking', even though he didn't know that that was what it would eventually be called. Using his increasing notoriety, plus the money from Isabella, he made a lot of influential friends, including a Duke called Don Luis de la Cerda Medina Celi. It was a long name, but the duke could afford it. He was very wealthy. Not only that, he liked Colón and he liked the sound of his Great Dream, which until now had been rapidly turning into a

DON LUIS DE LA CERDA MEDINA CELI

nightmare! In fact the duke was so impressed by Cris and his plan that he agreed to back it, to the tune of three or four thousand ducats. Now, I've no idea what that is in real money, but it sounds a lot. It was certainly enough to start building ships. They were to start work at the port of Santa Maria.

Out of courtesy, Duke ('Call me Don') Celi told his friends Ferdy and Issy about his sponsorship of Colón. Well! I imagine their noses were put so far out of joint that they'd have had to look over their shoulders to sniff, wouldn't you? I mean, here they are, the most powerful monarchs in the world, fresh from a war with Granada[47], got their own Inquisition and every-

---

[47] Not the English TV company, or the Ford car.

thing, just been voted Catholic Sovereigns by the Pope . . . I should think they felt well sick. But they couldn't show it. They couldn't just say: 'Oh, well, if you're gonna give him some dosh, Don, then I s'pose we might slip him some readies as well.'

No. That's not the way Royalty operated, not in the fifteenth century, anyway. But certainly they would have been keen to show themselves to be supportive. Apart from anything else, they now had Diego Colón and Cris's other little boy[48] working as Royal Pageboys. He was almost part of the family, really. So how did they handle it? Brilliantly. This is what happened:

The Catholic Sovereigns announced that they wished to reconsider their support of the Great Dream. Don Celi immediately withdrew his offer in deference to Their Majesties. Isabella then set up a Royal Commission to consider the plan (i.e. rubber-stamp it). To make it all look totally above board they really went to town. The Commission consisted of 3 Archbishops, 14 Bishops, 9 Dukes, 4 Marquesses, 10 Counts, and a Cardinal. (There was probably a tea lady as well, but I doubt if she was allowed to vote.)

It was now six years since Colón had last applied.

---

[48] Other little boy? Yes! Colón had a second son by his mistress (oo-er, missus!) Beatrice Havana (no relation to the cigars). She looked after him and kept him supplied with cash through the lean years. He certainly knew how to pick his ladies didn't he?

14 Bishops

10 Counts

9 Dukes

4 Marquesses

3 Archbishops

1 Cardinal

A partridge
in a pear tree

He had been banging his head against a brick wall all that time. Now, at last, success was in his grasp. And what did he do? He blew it! He totally, utterly and completely blew it!

Just as they were about to agree to help him, he pulled out a paper with five demands on it. They were the conditions under which he would accept their financial help. Anyone would think he was doing Their Majesties a favour. But that was the trouble – he thought he was! These were the conditions, which became known as the Santa Fe Capitulations:

1 That I Christóbal Colón, shall henceforth be known as Admiral of the Ocean sea, in such lands and continents as I might discover.

2 That I be Viceroy and Governor General over all sed lands and continents.

3 That I keep one tenth of all pearls, precious stones, gold, silver, spices, and all other articles and merchandise in whatever manner found, bought, bartered or gained within his Admiralty, the costs first deducted.

4 That I or my nominees should be sole judge in all disputes arising out of traffic between Spain and those countries I discover.

5 That I be entitled to contribute one eighth part of the expenses in fitting out vessels for this enterprise, and receive an eighth part of the profits.

You can tell he was a merchant, can't you[49]? Well, not surprisingly, Their Majesties sent him packing. No-one had ever spoken to them like that before. Well, that's not strictly true. Actually, dozens of people had spoken to them like that, and worse. But none of them had ever lived long enough to say: 'Only Joking!' Colón wasn't joking, though. He was deadly serious. So were they when they kicked him out of court.

Colón headed back to Palos, a dejected man. Had he been a songwriter he would probably have sat down and written a ballad full of the pain of the cup of fulfilment being snatched rudely from one's mouth, and the resulting heartbreak.

I GOT THOSE, THEY DONE GIVE ME THE SHOVE, AN' I AIN'T GOIN' DISCOVERIN' BLUES

---

[49] He was going to put in another demand for a badge or a special hat, but he decided against it. After all, no point in being greedy, is there?

And there it might have ended, except that some wise old courtier (it might have been Don Celi, it might not, it doesn't really matter) pointed out that Colón's demands weren't so outrageous, because:

A. IF HE DIDN'T COME BACK THEY'D BE OFF THE HOOK ANYWAY

B. IF HE CAME BACK EMPTY HANDED, IT WOULDN'T MATTER WHAT HE WANTED TO CALL HIMSELF BECAUSE THE REST OF THE WORLD (THE DISCOVERED BITS ANYWAY) WOULD BE CALLING HIM A COMPLETE PILCHARD

C. IF HE CAME BACK SUCCESSFUL, LADEN WITH GOLD, JEWELS AND GENERAL SPARKLY STUFF, THEN SPAIN WOULD BE SO RICH THAT THEY COULD AFFORD TO MAKE COLÓN THE QUEEN OF SHEBA.[50]

Whichever way you looked at it, Their Majesties couldn't possibly lose!

A messenger was sent to catch up with Our Hero and tell him that Their Majesties hand changed their minds. It took two weeks (he was a slow runner) but he delivered the message.

The trip was on!

---

[50] Unless, of course, there already was one.

Cause for Celebration – And Concern

Back in Palos the monks cracked open a case of disgusting communion wine to toast their hero. They made appalling wine. They made great jam, but that wasn't the stuff that celebration toasts are made of. It's more the stuff that jam toast is made of. Still, despite the burning in the throat and the distressing nausea, Cristóbal Colón was toasted on his way. It might indeed take three years. He might indeed never come back. But he was on his way!

However, he did have a slight problem. He wasn't much of a sailor! Oh, he understood navigation and was a very learned man when it came to charting and mapping, with a particular flair for inventing exotic islands that didn't exist. He was also a brilliant merchant and a natural leader, by all accounts. But he was no sailor. We know this to be true because in Colón's own diaries he quotes one of his crew as saying: 'If you're a good sailor, I'm a budgie!'

Colón had the offender locked in a small cage with his own mirror and bell, but it didn't alter the fact that when it came to sailing, our Cris was a non-starter. Oh, yes, he'd sailed dozens of times. But that doesn't make you good at it any more than the ability to fall asleep in the Houses of Parliament makes you a good politician. Or the speed of reflex to shout: 'Oh, no! We're gonna crash!' makes you a good driver. As long as his Great Dream remained just that, his lack of nautical ability wasn't a problem. Now that the voyage was becoming a reality, though, something needed to be done.

Enter, stage left, the nautical Pinzon Brothers!

He Ain't Heavy - He's My Brother (And so is He)

In 1492, if you were setting out to sail across an ocean that you personally believed to be at least three thousand miles across, you had to be either:

1 Completely mad
2 A brilliant sailor
or
3 Both

There is no evidence to suggest that Colón was mad. (Boring, self-opinionated, brilliant at conkers, lousy at dominoes, but not mad.) And, as we have just established, he was no sailor. So, if he was going to be even slightly successful in his venture, he was going to have to surround himself with some top-flight sailing muscle. And, much though it hurt him to admit it, that is exactly what he did. Fortunately, Palos, being a sea port, was full of sailors. Not all good, obviously, but even the bad ones were better than Cris.

There was one particular nautical family in Palos who knocked all other sailors into a cocked hat - the

Pinzon Brothers!
There was Martín (Martin),

Vicente (Vince),

and Francisco (Frank).

And they were the best. Everyone sang their praises. Even the monks, although they did it in Latin Plain-song. The Pinzons were the best, and they were available. All Colón had to do was to invite them to sail with him. But this was the problem. He hated anyone who was better than him. What if they showed him up? It's all very well being in charge, but there's not a lot of point in saying: 'Do as I say! I'm the boss!' when it's obvious you don't know what you're talking about!

If he was ever to realize his dream, Colón would have to swallow his pride. He also decided to swallow a few pints of the local brew, for good measure. He went to the local tavern, known to be a favourite with the Pinzon brothers, and waited. Of course, he didn't have to wait long. He was quite a local celebrity himself. Wherever he went, people would come up to him and say things like: 'Get out of my garden!' And more or less the same happened on his fateful Friday evening in the Ferret and Spinnaker. No sooner had he bought a pint and settled by the fire, than a large threatening voice said:

'You're sitting on my cap!'

Fortunately the person wasn't wearing it at the time. Colón retrieved the cap, spent a few frantic moments trying to clean it up (before realizing that it was meant to smell like that), and handed it back into the imposing hand of Martín Pinzon.

And thus the two great men finally met. It became clear from the beginning that they hated each other. Pinzon because Colón was so full of himself, Colón because Pinzon was so popular. To make matters worse, Martín had two brothers, Frank and Vince, who were equally fine sailors by all accounts, and equally popular.

After a few pints, Colón broached the subject of the voyage. Everyone listened in awed silence as he explained what he intended to do: to take three small ships three thousand miles across the Great Green Sea

Of Darkness, as the Atlantic was known then, and find the Western route to the East. He spoke of his dream, his vision, his calculations. He may even have pulled out his Satsuma-and-String working model. He left no detail out. He was a good talker. Well, he could keep it up for a long time without falling over, anyway. Once he had finished, he rested back in his seat and looked at the sea of weather-beaten faces surrounding his table in the corner of that tumble-down pub[51]. The silence was deafening.

Colón had long speculated what reaction he would get when he finally put his ideas to his potential crew – the people who would be actually doing the journey, not just paying for it. Would they be amazed? Envious? Greedy for the gold that he would surely find? What?

A myriad of possible reactions had flashed through his mind, but derisive laughter wasn't one of them. The building shook with it. Why, anyone would have thought that he'd told them his brother-in-law's favourite after-dinner story about the Pope, the trousers and the bowl of soup[52]!

The laughter cut into him like a knife. These base

---

[51] Only a few years later this same establishment became a Discovery Theme pub, offering a whole range of inter-bar activities, including a slave market on Thursdays.

[52] He did eventually try this anecdote out during a particularly frosty meal aboard the *Santa Maria*. He immediately wished he hadn't. Men of simple sea-faring stock like their humour basic. And anyway they hate religious gags.

fellows would never appreciate a Great Dream! However, in the words of the old Spanish proverb:

"Moor way than one there bee too take thy nife to the coat of a fluffy long earf"

Which, roughly translated, means 'there are more ways than one of skinning a rabbit'[53]. He also remembered the words of the other old Spanish proverb: *"Wot bee yon noif thy purf bee makin?"*

Which, again roughly translated, means: 'money talks!' So Colón introduced the assembled crew to the contents of his wallet and let them get acquainted. He soon had half his crew! But he was a businessman. He realized that this was no basis on which to run a venture such as he had in mind. If he had to pull his wallet out every time anyone questioned his authority, he was going to be flat broke before they even set sail! He needed a ploy, a ruse to ensure their respect and co-operation. He pulled out his conker.

Now conker matches were not a seaman's natural pastime, although they were quite popular in the ports, especially when blood was drawn. Colón was unbeaten. He challenged all comers. Everyone was quick to accept the challenge. They'd seen the inside of his wallet, remember? There was bound to be at least a drink in it for the winners. What did this city boy know about conkers? They were about to find out! Colón used his favourite, unbeaten *Pasali*, or 'Stonker-Conker'. It was a conker 3,879. Which,

---

[53] Unless you're a vegetarian.

when you consider most people don't get much above a conker 5, is pretty good. It was larger than average, as Cris had tended it lovingly for many years. In fact he had fed it so many artiticial nutrients that, if it had been an Olympic athlete, it would have failed a random drugs test the minute it got within thirty feet of an official.

The finer details of the evening are rather sketchy, since the winner of each competition[54] was brought a drink by the loser[55]. Suffice it to say that Colón woke up forty-eight hours later, with more than half his crew[56], a terrible hang-over, and an heart-felt pledge to never touch Old Dobbins Sierra Nevada Pale Ale ever again!

---

[54] Colón.
[55] Everyone else.
[56] Not in the same bed! I mean he'd signed them on for the trip!

Hello, Sailors !

While Cristóbal Colón oversaw the building of the ships and other important matters[57], the task of recruiting the rest of the crew fell to the Pinzon brothers. This really made sense. After all, the Pinzons knew most of the local talent, they were popular, and if anyone could persuade a load of superstitious sailors to go goodness knows where, for goodness knows how long, without much chance of getting back, Martin Pinzon could. Besides, this way saved Colón getting involved in any more conker and drinking competitions.

Pinzon understood the underlying driving force of your average fifteenth-century sailor – greed. So he spun them tales of exotic lands where houses had roofs made of gold and nobody had to wear a tie, and these simple sea-faring folk were soon signing up in droves. After all, anything was better than sitting around all day with your shirt undone, drinking ale and letting the sun beat on your navel . . . Hang on! That's not such a bad life! No! But if you could do all that on the

---

[57] Dinner parties with 'Ferdy' and 'Issy' (or I*ffy* as her nickname would have been, rather prophetically, written in those days.

front porch of a house with a golden roof, well! And, for some at least, the promise of getting out of jail sounded just the job!

'Out of jail?' I hear you say[58]. Yes! Because, believe it or not, some of the seamen were recruited from the local jail. Pinzon paid their fines and they joined the crew. After all, if you're about to sail into the unknown, you want to surround yourself with the very best, even if they are a bit light-fingered! Colón did not approve. Now, whether Pinzon recruited convicts in order to get back at Colón for a humiliating defeat at conkers, or whether he simply signed them up because they were the best, we will never know because history doesn't bother to tell us. All we know is that there were at least two murderers, seven pickpockets, one arsonist, two illegal street jugglers and a particularly bad actor[59] among the men and boys who filed aboard the ships on that fateful departure day in early August, 1492.

---

[58] or 'gaol', depending on your preference.
[59] He had been arrested not, as was usually the case, for illegal acting. He had a permit, but it was his acting that got him into trouble. The charge, when he was dragged in front of Justice Philipo (String 'Em Up And Don't Cut 'Em Down Even If They Promise Never To Do It Again) Sadistrianni, was:

'That he wilfully and with rehearsal murdered the verse of one of the plays of noted playsmith Plato the Greek. Plus, he wasn't the leest bit funny anyway either.'

But that day was still some weeks off. Cristóbal Colón still had to raise the remainder of the money to build the ships. Again, fate stepped in to lend a hand, in the shape of the good people of Palos. They were to solve part of Cris's financial problem, although they didn't yet know it!

The Good, The Bad, And The Ugly News!

The good news was that Ferdinand and Isabella had agreed to finance Colón's trip, or enterprise in the Indies as he now referred to it. The bad news was that they weren't that keen to pay the whole whack. True, Cris was paying an eighth of the cost himself, but that still meant that they would have to stump up a fairly sizeable 'wedge'. Something had to be done.

Now, if you were the king and queen you could do whatever you liked, but you had to 'appear' to be fair. Your actions had to have some basis in law. So the Catholic sovereigns got together all the best lawyers in the land and set them to work, trying to find a legal way of forcing someone else to chip in for Colón's trip. The lawyers were delighted. After all, a job like this could take years. And, at whatever outrageous daily rate lawyers charged then, they would all be able to retire to any one of the innumerable (non-existent) islands depicted on the latest maps. The Wood Pigeon Islands looked nice.

What the lawyers came up with was this: The people of Palos were to provide, at their own cost, two of the three ships, fully rigged and provisioned, within ten days, or else!

'Or else what?' enquired the belligerent townsfolk.

'Or else you'll all get locked up, that's what!'

And the legal basis for this rather high-handed action? It seems that the lawyers had come up with some ancient court case where several Palos men had been tried for smuggling and piracy. They had been found guilty, but sentence had never been passed for some reason. Maybe the judge had wanted to get home early or something.

Anyway, better late than never, eh? Though I doubt that the people of Palos looked at it that way. I imagine there was more than a bit of moaning. After all, Colón wasn't from round there, was he? He was from Genoa. On the other hand, Pinzon was going on the trip, and he was generally regarded as 'a bloomin' good bloke', so maybe it was O.K. after all. Doubtless this kind of banter went on in the inns, taverns, kitchens and parlours of Palos late into the night. Probably until dawn. Or at least until it 'dawned' on them that they could chat about it until they were blue in the face but they had no choice. The Catholic sovereigns had spoken, and there wasn't a single thing the people of Palos could do about it. So there.

The third ship had also been found, so now, Don Cristóbal Colón, the Admiral of the Ocean Sea[60] had

---

[60] He wasn't called Don as in: 'Hello, Don, how yer goin', mate?' Don was the Spanish equivalent of 'Sir'.

his fleet. Thus, on the eve of 2nd August 1492, the officers and crews of Colón's little band of brave men and boys filed into the church of Saint George at Palos to confess their sins and receive absolution.

The following morning Colón rose early and boarded the *Santa Maria*. He signalled the other ships to get underway. As the sun rose, the ships floated down the Rio Tinto on a becalmed sea, sails hanging limp. What a wonderful sight that must have been – the crowds standing on the quayside cheering as pickpockets relieved them of the troublesome weight of their purses. As you might imagine, two accounts exist of this event: the one in Brother Bartolome De Las Casas's *Columbus Diario*, and the true one in the *Colón Diaries*. Let's compare them. First Las Casas:

'Weighed anchor at sun-rise. Modest wind. Weather fair. Stood on bridge. Gave orders to move steady. Course West.

Now the Colón Diaries:

'Woken near out of bed by racket of chains. Diego sed twas the anchor. To be sure many rough fellows were pulling some big thing from the seebed. Went to stand by the big post with the cloth on it (mast) to get away from their infernal row. Told them to go that way and pointed. They seemed to understand.'

I know which account I believe!

As they passed the monastery at La Rabida, the monks could be heard chanting:

'Et nunc et in perpetuum'

'Evermore and evermore.'

And so it began. The Great Dream.

Soon the ships were dots on the horizon, and the people of Palos, who had helped make this historic journey possible, were left standing in wonder. As they watched the last tip of sail disappear from view, one thought was going through their collective brain: how did that crafty beggar Colón raise the rest of the cash?

A Mystery Solved

A TRIP OF A LIFETIME!!!

That's what the handbill said. And for Frank and Connie Escabados, it was just what they needed. Living in a house made almost entirely out of cow dung was no joke, unless you had a really weird sense of humour, but that's where they lived.

That's what the estate agent's blurb had said. And for Frank and Connie Escabados it was all they could afford. But at least they had a sort-of roof over their heads, even if they'd lost all their friends. In fact the only person who had ever visited their 'home' and referred to it as 'homely' was Peg Leg Jake, and as we already know his sense of smell wasn't his strong point[61]. He had visited the Escabadoses to tell them

---

[61] Jake didn't in fact have a strong point. He did, however, have a strong smell.

that they were the lucky winners. Yes! They had successfully filled in their name and address without any smudges. They had completed the sentence, in not more than as many words as it took: 'I would like a free boat trip to a two-week all-expenses-paid-by-me holiday in the Canaries because . . .' And they'd enclosed a large sum of money.

As indeed had numerous other people. In fact the competition was a great success – one of Cristóbal Colón's better ideas. Everyone said that. Lewis de Torres, interpreter and bird impressionist, even went so far as to suggest that they forget the Voyage of Discovery and go into the competition business instead[62]. And so the Escabadoses were on their way. It was all fixed. Now all Jake had to fix was the rudder on the *Pinta* so that it would jump its gudgeons[63] halfway between Palos and the Canaries!

And so it was that the journey started on 3rd August[64] and stopped two weeks later while Colón sent the *Pinta* to Las Palmas, in Gran Canaria, for repairs, and the rest of the crew, including Francisco and Conchita Escabados, spent two sun-soaked weeks

---

[62] He suffered greatly from sea-sickness and was intelligent enough to realize that they were not going to be able to swim ashore every five minutes for warm badger's blood.

[63] Whatever they are.

[64] My mother's birthday, incidentally. I think, as a birthday treat, my father might have taken her to the quayside at Palos to wave them off.

on La Gomera, also in the Canary Isles. So it was that the trip got paid for!

And so it was that, on 6th September 1492, rested and replenished, the fleet finally weighed anchor in the Old World for the last time, and set sail for the New.

The Admiral of the Ocean Sea gave his course to the other captains, Martin and Vince Pinzon:

'West, gentlemen! Nothing to the north! Nothing to the south! West! West! West!'

And west it was.

But just who were those brave souls who were risking life, limb, and a nice steady nine-to-five job back in Palos packing fish? I think it's time we met them, don't you?

It's time to turn to the *Colón Diaries* for the fine detail . . .

Peeps At The Diaries

Peg leg Jake

Once the voyage was truly under way, Colón started committing his thoughts to paper on a daily basis. Before that, I suppose, he'd been too busy. But now that the experts were running the ship, all he had to do was stand around looking important and be sick every now and then.

The *Colón Diaries* provide, I believe, a real insight into what it must have been like to sail into the unknown. We also have the benefit of Jake's comments, scribbled in the margin of the original diaries, rather in the style of De Facia, the thirteenth-century Italian graffiti artist, and the first man to be hanged for doodling in a library book[65].

But how, some Doubting Thomases might ask, did a simple Able Seaman such as Jake get close enough to an Admiral of the Ocean Sea in order to have sight of

---

[65] This is still a capital offence, by the way!

the diaries, let alone 'rescue' them for posterity? Well, it would be lovely to be able to tell you a tale of deep friendship, bridging the intellectual gap and scaling the class barrier. Alas, this is not the case. As we will see from the diaries, Columbus did not make friends easily, although he lost them quickly enough. No, the Admiral tolerated Jake. He had no choice. Jake caught him cheating at Scrabble. (Well, perhaps cheating is an overstatement. But if you call the creative use of Latin to get high scores when you're the only player who understands the language, 'cheating', then Colón cheated.) And Jake, taking his turn as waiter in the Officer's Mess[66], saw it happen.

---

[66] A 2 metre by 1 metre cupboard under the foc's'le, wherever that is.

Colón hotly denied cheating. He called it '*putting his education to good use*', but he obviously felt badly enough about it to need to keep Jake from spreading it around the rest of the crew.

Thus it was that Jake enjoyed the unique position of freedom of the Admiral's cabin and was able to get sight of Colón's innermost thoughts via the pages of his diaries. Later he was able to get hold of the diaries themselves and replace them with an exact copy, meticulously forged to such a degree that the two documents were indistinguishable from each other, the only differences being:

   1 By the time Jake's copy came into my possession it had his comments all over it.

   2 It has a smell that is unmistakeably Jake.

Thus it is that we are now able to solve many of the mysteries that have foxed historians[67] for centuries. Where relevant I have used Jake's comments alongside those of Cristóbal Colón. I have also compared the entries of the *Diaries* with those in the *Diario*. This more than proves my point that the Las Casas document is as made up as his name. But don't take my word for it. Judge for yourself!

---

[67] And helped them publish books and win Nobel prizes.

I Saw Three Ships

If we are going to try and re-live, through the pages of this book, the feelings and misgivings that Colón and his crew must have experienced, the first thing we need to know is the details of his boat and crew, isn't it? All right, let's look at Colón's boat. And here we are helped by the additional comments of Colón (in brackets) the diplomatic leader, and those of Jake (in italics) the plain-speaking bigot.

The *Santa Maria* was Colón's flagship. But although he travelled in this ship, he never really liked her. The feeling was mutual. She was hired from Juan de la Costa, who also sailed as the ship's master. The rest of the crew were:

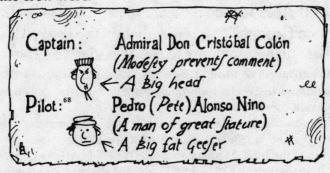

Captain: Admiral Don Cristóbal Colón
(*Modesty prevents comment*)
← *A Big head*

Pilot:[68] Pedro (*Pete*) Alonso Nino
(*A man of great stature*)
← *A Big fat Geeser*

---

[68] They had a pilot on board just in case the ship ever got airborne.

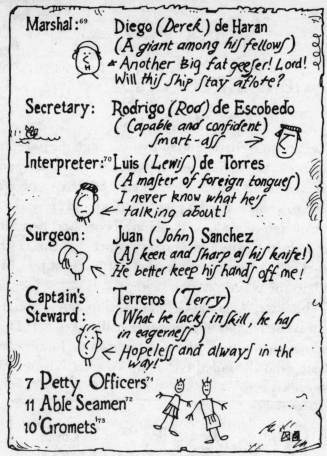

Marshal:[69] Diego (Derek) de Haran
(A giant among his fellows)
← Another Big fat geeser! Lord!
Will this ship stay afloat?

Secretary: Rodrigo (Rod) de Escobedo
(Capable and confident)
smart-ass →

Interpreter:[70] Luis (Lewis) de Torres
(A master of foreign tongues)
I never know what he's
← talking about!

Surgeon: Juan (John) Sanchez
(As keen and sharp as his knife!)
← He better keep his hands off me!

Captain's
Steward: Terreros (Terry)
(What he lacks in skill, he has
in eagerness)
← Hopeless and always in the
way!

7 Petty Officers[71]
11 Able Seamen[72]
10 'Gromets'[73]

---

[69] Similarly they had a marshal in case of trouble. The Americans still retain the term to this very day. Now you know where it comes from.

[70] Lewis was a Jew who spoke fluent Arabic. Colón felt that this would come in handy when talking to the Chinese when they reached the Indies! Languages never WERE his strong point.

[71] It was a stroke of bad luck for Colón that all the officers turned out to be really petty.

[72] He was luckier with the sailors, all of whom were very able.

[73] Elizabethan word for ship's boy or apprentice.

Now, forty may seem a small number for a ship's crew, but not when you realize that the ship was only 85 feet long!

Colón had little or no comment to make about his crew. It's unlikely that he had much to do with them at all. He had even less to say about the other two ships, The *Pinta* and the *Nina*, partly because he wasn't captaining them, but mainly because the Pinzon brothers *were*! You'll find the details of these ships and crews in the back of the book (Appendix 2).

In all there were just 90 men and boys, crammed into three small ships.

Or were there?

The Fourth Ship

It has always been assumed that there were only three ships on Colón's historic first journey of discovery. Indeed, Colón himself in the *Colón Diaries* is quoted as saying:

'We had three ships.'

And he was right. However, elsewhere in the diary is the strange entry:

'I'm sure we're being followed!'

And he was right about that, too.

So, who was following them? The answer is simple: the media! Yes! Even then a famous person couldn't blow their nose or set out to cross the Atlantic for the first time ever without the media wanting to muscle in on the act. So, who exactly were these people? I'll tell you:

The ship was a caravel, similar in size and weight to the *Nina*. Her given name was the *Santa Scholastica*. She was named after Saint Scholastica, the patron saint of convulsive children, but her crew referred to her as the *Oscar*. The crew were:

Captain	Celellio (Cecil) Berto de Mille
Master	Francisco (Frank) Coppola
Pilot	B. Gulls
Marshal	Matteo (Matt) Dilan
Surgeon/Barber	Maestre (Mr) Teesiweesi
Interpreter[74]	Silvesta Stallone
Secretary[75]	Stephano (Steven) Spilbirg
3 Able Seamen	
10 Acting Seamen[76]	
15 Artists	
Total crew: 35	

In addition there were make-up artists, lighting designers, casting consultants, stunt doubles, stand-ins, walk-ons (speaking), walk-ons (non-speaking), grips, best boys, runners, personal assistants, hangers-on, bar staff, outside caterers and everything else you might expect. Plus a few that you might not! You'll notice that there are no 'gromets' listed. This is because basically they were all gromets, or apprentices. They didn't really know one end of the boat (sorry – ship!) from the other. So what were they doing there? Well, they were making the Flicker-Book version of the trip. That's why there were fifteen artists on board, frantically painting everything as it happened, and getting the actors and crew to re-stage

---

[74] Doubling as dialogue coach.
[75] Script writer
[76] Hired more for their acting ability than their seamanship.

anything they missed. What a wonderful idea! What an amazing piece of history, captured as it happened!

Sadly, this wonderful document no longer exists. If it did it would provide a brilliant insight into the trip, as seen from an outsider's point of view. What happened to it? Did it get washed over the side by a freak wave? Destroyed by fire? Accidentally eaten by one of the actors[77] at the end-of-voyage party? No. It simply never got completed. Some say it went over budget, some say that the Captain spent most of the voyage getting the artists to paint sunsets. Others, less kindly, say that the artists spent most of the trip re-painting the leading actor's cabin in varying shades of puce every time he threw a 'wobbly'. Still others say that they can't remember anything from the time they embarked to the time they fell off in the New World.

But I can reveal precisely what became of this rag-bag of talent: they crossed the New World overland to the West Coast, renamed themselves Columbus Flicker-Books, and set about making cowboy and Indian pictures.

So, disappointingly, we don't have anything of theirs that we can use as a reliable reference. We do, though, have the *Colón Diaries*. And through these marvellous documents we can discover for the very first time what it was really like on that First Voyage of Discovery.

One thing emerges very clearly: it was no picnic!

---

[77] Let's face it, actors will eat anything!

We Are Sailing, We Are Sailing[78]

The journey from the Canaries to San Salvador[79] was long. Very long. Nearly five weeks. Which is a very long time to be cooped up in three small ships[80]. And, of course, there weren't only men and boys aboard. Oh, no! Each boat was heavily laden with enough supplies for a three-month voyage. This must have surprised the crews, because Cristóbal Colón had managed to persuade them that the trip would only take a couple of weeks[81]. So, apart from the crews, what was there on board?

THE CARGO

Food and drink, mainly. Barrels of salt beef, ships' biscuits[82], wine to take away the taste of the biscuits, rum to take away the taste of the wine, soap, razors,

---

[78] Oddly enough, about the only thing this voyage lacked was Rod Stewart!

[79] As Colón insisted on renaming it. The locals were perfectly happy with the name that the island had already, Ghanahani. They were also furious at the local post office.

[80] Aboard the *Oscar* time seemed to fly. But then it was party, party, party, all the way.

[81] He was to live to regret this little deception.

[82] Which came complete with maggots for extra iron.

deodorant, Old Spice aftershave[83] and fresh water. (After all, they couldn't drink the sea, not unless they wanted to be seriously sick. Then, of course, there were the gifts to impress any natives they might meet: beads, bits of coloured glass, hawk bells and hoods,[84] coloured cloth, pins and needles, old copies of *Sailor's Own*, nodding dogs, musical tie carousels, door chimes – in fact any old useless junk that might impress someone with the brain of a belt-loop[85].

Ordinary sailors were only allowed to take what they stood up in, but Officers could take personal items: lithographs of the kids, Travel Scrabble, that sort of thing. All of which didn't leave an awful lot of space for living quarters[86]. So how did they cope with, say, sleeping? Well, as the illustration on the next page shows, Colón had a bedroom with en-suite facilities, monogrammed towels, the lot. But then he was the Admiral of the Ocean Sea.

---

[83] To take away the taste of the rum!

[84] Wow! Gimmee, Gimmee!

[85] Another bad move on Colón's part was assuming that anyone who went around half naked with emulsion paint sploshed around their face was stupid. The explorer James Cook made the same mistake in Hawaii, but he didn't live to regret it.

[86] In view of the lack of space, they should probably be called living sixteenths.

The senior officers slept in cupboards. Everyone else slept wherever they could. Old Salts who knew the ropes avoided sleeping on them as they were very uncomfortable. Instead they would bag their spot around about cocoa-and-bedtime-story time, and put their hats on it. Then they would sleep in their hats. The wiser of the Spanish seamen wore very large hats, called *slumbreros*, which of course is the original version of the Mexican sombrero. They would sleep

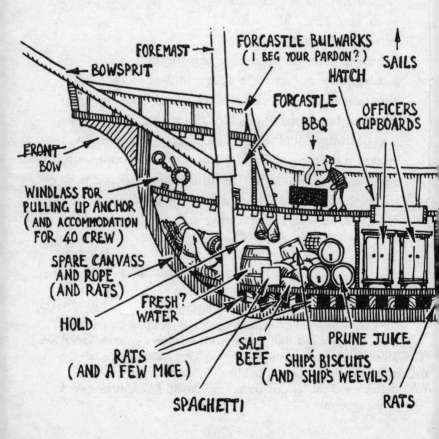

FOREMAST →

FORCASTLE BULWARKS
(I BEG YOUR PARDON ?)

SAILS

← BOWSPRIT

HATCH

FORCASTLE
BBQ
↓

OFFICERS
CUPBOARDS

FRONT
BOW

WINDLASS FOR
PULLING UP ANCHOR
(AND ACCOMMODATION
FOR 40 CREW)

SPARE CANVASS
AND ROPE
(AND RATS)

FRESH?
WATER

HOLD

RATS
(AND A FEW MICE)

SALT
BEEF

PRUNE JUICE

SHIPS BISCUITS
(AND SHIPS WEEVILS)

SPAGHETTI

RATS

standing up if need be. The only problem with this was that the weevils from the ship's biscuits (the ones that didn't get eaten) also liked to curl up in the hats. This meant that, unless you wanted to be scratching all night, you had to stamp on your hat before you bedded down for the night. Colón observed this, and took it to be some strange custom popular among Spanish sailors.

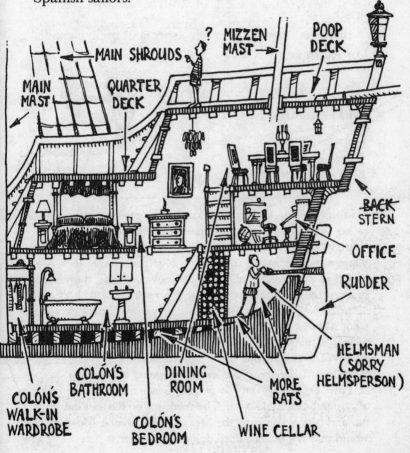

He was Italian, remember? In his diary he tells us:

"These spaniards are strange bed-fellows.[87] *They do danse upon there hats after they have done their prayers*[88] *and bisness.*[89] *Although noisie and unGodly, it cood catch on!"*[90]

At any rate, bedtime on board ship was always a bit of a free-for-all, often resulting in serious injury, even death.

But what about the other aspects of their lifestyle? For example:

THE LAVATORY

This consisted of a plank strapped to the side of the

---

[87] I think we can take this to mean strange fellows at bedtime, rather than strange fellows to share a bed with!

[88] Although these were deeply religious times, prayer for most old seadogs meant putting their hands together, closing their eyes and then counting to about 46, or however long they might imagine the average prayer to last, then squinting to check that no priest was watching them before they opened their eyes and went about their ungodly business. Although there were no priests on this particular voyage, most of the crew still counted to 46 out of force of habit.

[89] Ablutions. See the above section on going to the toilet!

[90] This was one of the few occasions when Colón was right, although he didn't know it. The stamping on the hats did catch on, and is now known as the Mexican Hat Dance. Most sailors would now not be seen dead doing it, however.

boat. Anyone feeling the need dropped their trousers and sat on the plank. And that really did apply to everyone, including Admirals. According to the diaries, one enterprising seaman made a nice sideline out of selling T-shirts bearing the slogan: *I've seen Cristóbal Colón's Bottom.*

Naturally Colón was unhappy about this arrangement. His diary tells us:

I wiſh I cood go about my biſneſſ without the rougher element looking at my private partſ

He may have found small comfort in the fact that most of the crew who observed him agreed that this was about the only thing the Admiral did properly! It would have been even less comfort to learn that the others were only watching him so that they could tell their grandchildren that they saw him fall into the sea! All in all, it was a haphazard business! As was:

COOKING

The *Colón Diaries* tell us:

A fire waſ litted on a bed of ſand inſide a wooden box

Now, you don't have to be a Fire Prevention Officer to work out the risks inherent in this particular system. Emilio Sanchez, the arsonist and part-time dolphin rustler referred to earlier, was excused cooking on account of his medical condition, but you didn't need an arsonist chef to put the whole ship at risk. A quick change of wind direction, and you can imagine the dialogue on the bridge:

COLÓN: Something smells good.
MASTER: Yes, Admiral. I think it's the quarter deck!

Not that there was an enormous difference in the taste of the food once it was cooked. Although I suppose burnt salt beef is marginally less disgusting than raw. The ship's biscuits weren't much better. They were so full of maggots that the crew used to place them on the decks and have biscuit races. The *Diaries* record Peralonso Nino having his biscuit disqualified on the grounds that it was over ninety per cent protein.

But cookery was not the only area of duty in which the crew played with fire. There was also:

SIGNALLING

Naturally the ships needed to keep in touch with each other, even though they all knew which way they were going. Apart from helping the general camaraderie of the event, it also gave them the chance to hold inter-ship biscuit races and other tedium-busting events. Now, under normal circumstances they could have shouted to each other, but the *Nina* and the *Pinta* were much faster than the *Santa Maria*, and the Pinzon brothers liked to race ahead and then wait for the *Santa Maria* to catch up. This served two purposes: it relieved some of the boredom, and it also helped demonstrate to Colón who were the better sailors. (Not that he needed reminding, but they liked to rub his nose in it.) We mustn't forget, of course, that there was also a prize for the first person to sight land. A prize which, incidentally, Colón kept for himself. But more of that later.

Since they couldn't shout, and no-one had yet had the foresight to invent semaphore, naval signalling flags, or the Aldis lamp, just how did they communicate? Let's check in the *Diaries*:

ſmoke ſignalſ

Yes. Fmoke Fignalf. I mean, smoke signals! That's probably how the American Indians got the idea. You

123

see, Colón's trip wasn't a complete waste of time. They lit a fire in the stern of the ship, then doused or fanned it, depending on the message. They had a set of signals similar to Morse code, the principal ones being:

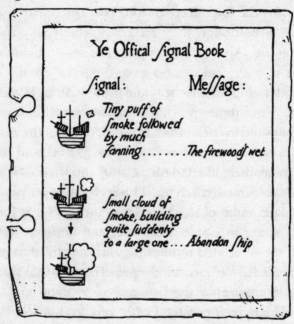

There were many others, of course, such as: 'What time is it? My sundial's stopped', but these were only used in real emergencies, or when the boredom factor reached Let's-throw-Colón-over-the-side pitch. Actually, that pitch was reached quite early on. Jake comments in the Diaries that it was reached " *Juft afor we leaved Palof* "

But why, I hear you say, didn't Colón invent a better system of signalling? After all, wasn't this the man who had invented the Loafer?[91] It certainly was! And he certainly did invent, or at least attempt to invent, a better system of signalling. Referring to the *Diaries* again:

> '*I proposed that a series of flags*[92], *of differing hues*[93] *shud be affixed unto poles, and waved thereon to other fellows, that wud wave them back.*'

Not such a silly idea. A similar system was eventually adopted by the navy. There was, however, one big drawback with this system as far as Colón was concerned: he was colour-blind. Therefore, the waving of different-coloured flags as a means of communication left him totally confused. What added to his confusion was a strange twist of fate that meant that whatever combination the flags were waved in, as far as Colón was concerned the message always read: But I haven't even *got* a mackerel. You might imagine that he would have thought of this before he set about using the system. But no. He was far too keen to endear himself to his fellow sailors, who were rapidly going off him.

---

[91] *Loafer?* Yes, indeed. For the monks at San Lucia de la Ministroni had sold the secret of their Broth-Crêpes (at an enormous profit) to the local bakers, who had re-named the shoe the *Loafer* after their produce!

[92] I assume he means Flags!

[93] I assume he means Colour. There was no-one called Hugh on board the ship.

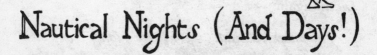

Nautical Nights (And Days!)

But apart from eating and going to the toilet, there was of course the actual sailing of the vessels. This involved a certain amount of pulling up the sails and lowering the sails, as the wind conditions changed. Or in Colón's case, as he changed his mind[94]. As with everything our Cris did, he had his own unique form of instructing the crew. Here are some examples of how a proper ship's captain would instruct his crew in those days, and how Colón did it:

REAL CAPTAIN:	COLÓN:
Hoist the mains'l! Trim off the Mizz'n!	Quicker!
Steady she goes! Awa' Foss'l!	Slower!
Muster a quarterdecks! Hard on capstan, me hearties	Stop!

---

[94] Or when Juan de la Costa whispered in his ear that if he went to full sail now the wind would snap the ship in two.

I think I prefer Colón's version. Except, of course, his orders normally came out more like:

"Quicker! No, Slower! No, change that! I was right the . . . stop a minute. Left. Right. Er . . . which hand do I hold my fork in?"

Luis de Torres was given the task of interpreting these instructions, which only made them more confusing, because he could only interpret Arabic. Still it all helped to amuse the crew, and keeping them amused was a full time job. After all, once you've got the sails the way you need them, changed them a few times, then put them back again, had a laugh at one of the officers going to the loo, had a biscuit race, fricasséed the poop deck and tried to invent smoke signals for all your favourite dirty words, there wasn't a lot else to do.

According to the *Columbus Diario*, the most exciting thing that happened was spotting a big patch of seaweed[95]. This terrified the crew *'beyond there witf end,'*

---

[95] At least in those days you could be sure that it *was* seaweed. These days it's far more likely to be raw sewage. On second thoughts, given the toilet arrangements in those days . . .

according to de las Casas. Apparently they thought that it was going to eat them or something. Four tons of killer seaweed was going to crawl into the boat and devour them, or turn them into zombies with their heads on back to front. They'd been looking at too many late-night flicker-books. As it was, the seaweed was quite content to drift on being seaweed. That's the trouble with most marine plant life – no ambition! Oh yes, the wrecking of the *Santa Maria* was marginally more exciting than the seaweed, but the excitement was tempered with the worry of how they were all going to get back to 'civilization' in two small ships.

History relates how Colón deliberately misled the crew about the distance they had travelled each day. He would knock a few knots off the daily distance, in order to give the impression that they weren't travelling that far. He felt that the crew would be up in arms if they realized just how far they had gone. Here he seriously miscalculated their mood.[96] Frankly, they wouldn't have minded how far they travelled as long as they got there soon. Those who believed the earth was flat wouldn't have minded falling off the edge, as long as it happened sooner rather than later.

Have you ever been on a really long car journey? One where your little brother keeps saying: 'Are we there yet?' He usually starts just as you pull out of your own front drive, and stays stuck in that groove for the rest of the journey. Before long, you're not the only one getting badly affected. Dad starts suggesting games to pass the time – Battleships with real guns or Hangman with real string.

Well, the journey to the New World was exactly like that, only multiplied by the number of crew. And it was Colón's job to do something about it. After all, he was the Boss. He was the one who'd forgotten to employ an Entertainments Manager. He wasn't helped by the fact that one of the crew of the *Nina*, Filippo (Mad Dog) Pellew, had developed a very rare

---

[96] He also miscalculated the distances, and was in fact giving the crew the actual distance travelled, not an invented one! (*fact*)

condition with a Latin name that would require an entire chapter to itself, but one that would have delighted Cristóbal Colón, had I the wit and Latin skill to write it. This condition, which normally only struck seafarers and property developers, manifested itself in the sudden and uncontrollable desire to shout 'LAND AHOY!' This he did with increasing regularity, until his fellow crew members managed to take his mind off it by telling him, in great anatomical detail, what they would do to him if he didn't shut up.

If something wasn't done, and done quickly, to relieve the tension, someone would be going for a very, very, very long swim.

And his first name began with 'C'.

And his second name began with 'C' too.[97]

---

[97] CC: you can tell he was Italian!

Rallying to the Flag (Ship)

So how did Colón prevent a mutiny? Well, there were the conker matches, of course. But since he was unbeatable they soon tired of those. Then there was Scrabble for the Officers, but as we have already seen, Colón was given to using an unfair advantage[98]. I Spy was popular for a while, but since it required a very basic knowledge of the alphabet and the imagination to spot an object, think of a letter and match the two together, there were very few members of the crew who could join in. Selecting an invented island and crossing it off the map when you didn't come to it became quite popular for a while, but since Colón had been responsible for inventing some of them himself in his map-drawing days, it wasn't considered diplomatic to play it too often.

There were those who argued that, since Colón wasn't coming up with any great ideas himself, they would have to make their own amusement. They had long since tired of his juggling. Keel-hauling was no fun, because you only saw the poor frightened wretch

---

[98] i.e. Latin.

before he went in the water, and his remains when he came back out and you never actually saw him being hauled along the keel. As a spectator sport it had a lower rating than sumo wrestling, or Indian football. Besides, there weren't really enough crew to waste on blood sports.

Polishing the decks became popular for a while. Colón had a passion for cleanliness[99], and liked to be able to see his face in the decks, not realizing of course that untreated wood has little or no reflective qualities. Still, as Jake observes in the margin of the diaries:

> *Old Cris was a stickler, he was. Hee liked all things shipshape and Bristol fashun, and thats thee Gods Honest truth of it, to bee sure.*[100]

---

[99] He was in the wrong profession, then!

[100] Not that Jake would have spotted the truth if it had been eighteen feet tall and walked into the room wearing a large orange hat and a badge, . . .

One thing Colón did set his mind to during the voyage was developing his 'shoe with the sticky bottom', or *Tre-Hon-Aere*, for use at sea. There was a barrel of mastic aboard the *Santa Maria* and Cris was never without it, being a great believer in its abilities to hold things together[101]. All he needed was material for the 'man-made' uppers: canvas. Well, there was plenty of that around, wasn't there? Why, it was everywhere you looked, as long as you were looking up. He quickly put the disgruntled crew to work cutting shoe-shaped holes in the sails[102], then stitching them together. After that they were dipped in the mastic, to make perfect deck shoes.

---

[101] Were he alive today, he would be the sort of person who carries a tube of superglue everywhere, and can never get his hands out of his pockets.

[102] Which slowed the ship down somewhat.

The shoes were a big hit with the crew – the most exciting thing that had happened to some of them, by all accounts.[103] Why, some of the 'gromets' couldn't wait for them to dry before they tried them on, and promptly stuck to the deck! But what could they call them? 'Broth-crêpes' was fine for the monks of the Holy Order of the Bowl, but it wouldn't do for sailors. Colón suggested naming them after a part of the ship and, since he was in charge, everyone agreed. But which part? Their smell (particularly after the sailors had been wearing them for five minutes) suggested they should be called Bilge Pumps, but Colón eventually settled on plimsolls,[104] so plimsolls it was.

It was during this interlude, which the diaries refer to as shoe-phoria, that land was sighted. Or perhaps one should say that 'Mad Dog' Pellew, over on the *Nina*, yelled 'Land Ahoy' amd got himself thrown over the side. Legend tells us that he swam to the *Oscar*, which was still following at this point, and later became a famous Flicker Book star.

And so the honour of sighting land fell to one Rodrigo de Triana aboard the *Pinta*, as he climbed up to feed the crows. He turned away to avoid a particularly nasty peck, and accidentally saw land.

---

[103] Life can be tedious when you're a simple sailor with the brain of a bicycle pump.

[104] after the 'Plimsoll line' which was a row of nails along the outside of the hull where the seaman traditionally hung their socks to air.

Before he knew where he was, he was falling to the deck[105]. Martin Pinzon, captain of the *Pinta*, looked up in response to de Triana's cry of 'Aah!' as he fell past the captain's ear, and so he too spotted land[106].

They were finally here. After five weeks at sea, 748 conker matches, 60 games of Scrabble[107], assorted games of I Spy and Hunt The Pudding and, of course, the biscuit races, they had reached land.

Of course, the Pinzon Brothers had known for some time that land was near. They had looked over the side and seen twigs and bits of foliage floating in the sea. It must have been very exciting, rather like hearing the first cuckoo of Spring. That's the sort of thing that makes you want to write to the papers:

Dear Sirs,
I have just spotted a twig floating in the Atlantic ocean. Does this mean that we are nearing land, or is my boat dropping to bits?
Yours,
Worried of Palos.

---

[105] Actually, before he knew where he was he was in the ship's hospital cupboard, with the surgeon barber, Mr Derek, standing over him. Mr Derek had no idea how to treat him, so he just gave him a perm and tint.

[106] 'Confirmed the sighting' history prefers to call it!

[107] 60, that is, if you, don't count the hundreds of games that were abandoned because Colón confiscated the board and went to bed in a sulk.

Colón hadn't looked over the side. He was too busy revamping his shoe. So the announcement came as something of a surprise to him.

But where were they exactly?

'The Indies,' announced Cristóbal Colón, very sure of himself. And he remained convinced of this fact until his dying day[108]. This explains why he called the locals 'Indians'.[109]

He was actually in the Bahamas, on a tiny island called *Ghanahani*. He put to shore, planted his flag, and renamed the island San Salvador, which means Holy Saviour. And the island had indeed been his saviour. One more week at sea and he would have been fishpaste. The novelty of the shoes was wearing off.

WE PRAISE ALMIGHTY GOD FOR OUR DELIVERANCE TO THIS PLACE WHICH WE RIGHTLY CLAIM AS LEGAL POSSESSION IN THE NAME OF THIER ROYAL HIGHNESSES QUEEN ISABELLA AND KING FERDINAND OF ARRAGON AND CASTILE

[108] Probably beyond his dying day, for all we know. He might even have been reincarnated as a daisy, telling every passing bee foolish enough to listen: 'I discovered the Western route to the Indies, you know!'

[109] And why they called him a prat.

The locals really didn't know what to make of him, any more than he knew what to make of them. If these were orientals, they were a far cry from the sophisticated types Marco Polo[110] had described. No matter. He had more pressing things to attend to. Through Luis de Torres, the interpreter, Colón tried to find out:

1 the whereabouts of the Ruler of the Orient, the Great Khan[111]
2 the whereabouts of their gold.

But not necessarily in that order. Torres was more than a bit put out when he discovered that the islanders didn't speak Arabic, and he resorted to that other form of communication one uses when trying to

HUH?

---

[110] Marco Polo had journeyed to the Orient some years earlier, bringing back tales of a sophisticated people who printed books and burned coal. Nobody believed him at first. He later went on to invent the first mint with a hole in it.
[111] They'd got a letter for him.

get through to foreigners, Very Loud Shouting, which he was particularly fluent in. It seemed to do the trick. The local chief, spokesperson or whatever he was, told them through sign language that they didn't have any gold but he felt sure they'd have plenty on the next island. As for the Great Khan, he'd never heard of him. Was he in the Benny Hill Show? None too happy about this, Colón nevertheless thanked him, took six natives hostage[112], and journeyed to the next island, the one with all the gold on.

He arrived later that day, claimed it as the property of Spain and renamed it Santa Maria de la Concepción. This proved a bit of a mouthful for the locals, who spoke no Spanish but were happy to give it a bash, so the ever-practical English later renamed it Rum Cay. Much better, don't you think? Anyway, on this island too the locals seemed friendly but bemused. They hadn't got any gold, it was all on the next island just up the road a piece. However, they were delighted with the treasures that Colón had very generously bought for them:

'You shouldn't have! No, really! It was too kind!' they kept telling him in sign language. 'It's so embarrassing that we haven't got any gold for you, especially after you've brought us all these . . . whatever they are. Have you tried the island up the road?' they waved at our hero.

***

[112] Sorry! I mean as guides. Free to come and go as they pleased as long as they didn't leave the ship.

My secret theory is that the natives saw all this junk – the hawk bells, the coloured glass beads, the signed etchings of Queen Isabella – for what it was, but were too polite to tell Colón what he could do with it all. They just sent him off to the next island instead! Tambourine jingles! That was another thing they gave them! Mind you, they're like gold-dust – ones that work, anyway.

So Cristóbal Colón went from island to island, renaming them: Crooked Island, Long Island, Fortune Island. He planted the Spanish flag and spread his largesse, and the welcome everywhere was as open and friendly as that which the newly-named San Salvadorians[113] had given him. But no gold was to be found.

Seeing that he was disappointed, the natives showed him some rolled-up leaves which they set fire to, then put between their lips to inhale the smoke. They called it *tobacco*. But Colón wasn't interested. It would never catch on.

---

[113] Who even now were trying to get used to their sudden change of nationality.

139

HAPPINESS IS A CIGAR
CALLED HAMMOCK

However, he did discover that the natives slept in hammocks, which seemed a very worthwhile alternative to the floor for a weary sailor,[114] so the trip hadn't been a complete wash-out.

Martin Pinzon caught on to what the natives were up to straight away. He decided to take the *Pinta* and explore for himself.

Colón was too wrapped up in his quest for gold to notice, and he was getting impatient. The natives took him in their dugout canoes to an island they called Colba (Cuba), which strangely enough he didn't give a silly name. But still no gold.

How could he possibly return to Spain without it? What would people say?

'You went all the way around the world, and all you've come back with is a folding bed you tie to a tree! Do us a favour!'

But at the eleventh hour[115] Colón found his prize – an island he renamed La Isla Española 'The Spanish Isle' and he found his gold.

Now he could go home. His mission was complete and he could return in triumph. Well, he could . . . but he was about to become one ship short.

---

[114] Not that he'd ever slept on the floor.
[115] Just before Christmas, actually.

HO HO HO!

On Christmas Day in the Morning

'I spy with my little eye something beginning with C.R.'

It was Christmas morning, and the watch were relieving their boredom. After all, what were they watching for? Pirates? What? There was nobody for miles but natives, and they were so friendly they'd give you their last cigar. That's why they were playing I Spy.

'C.R. . . . C.R. . . . that's a tricky one. C.R. . . .'

Everyone else was asleep in their new hammocks. The natives had given them as early Christmas presents. Not that the natives celebrated Christmas, but they would. You'll see. Cristóbal Colón would mount a second expedition, bring a few churchmen with him, and get these heathens sorted out. Knock a bit of religion into them. Stop them smoking – filthy habit!

'Give in?'

'No! Hang on! C.R. Cor, it's a tricky one and no mistake.'

Cristóbal Colón, dreaming of glory, slept in his bed. He'd thought of trying a hammock, but he didn't really want the lower ranks to get the wrong idea. Captains slept in clean sheets and sailors hung from the yardarm, and that's the way it would always be.

'Come on. We haven't got all night!'

'It's already day!'

'All day then. Have a guess.'

'C.R. No. It's got me foxed and no mistake.'

'Give in?'

'Yeah. What is it, this C.R., then?'

'Coral reef.'

'Coral reef? Where?'

'There. We're just about to . . . oh, blimey!'

The impact caused Cristóbal Colón to fall out of his bed on to the floor. That wouldn't have happened in a hammock.

The Rovers Return

It's always sad when you have to leave somewhere. It's sad for the leaver, but it's also sad for those who are left. Especially if they thought they were going too! And this is how it was for the crew of the recently shipwrecked *Santa Maria*.

The exact circumstances of her running aground on a coral reef are rather sketchy to say the least. Some are convinced that it happened exactly as I described. Others quote the evidence of Columbus's own invention, an early forerunner of the 'black box' flight recorder[116], where we hear the watch say:

'Oh, go on, Luis, let the Admiral drive! It *is* Christmas, after all!'

Which puts our Cris at the helm. Either way, he was heading home one ship short. The *Santa Maria*, which he'd never liked though he would never say that to Juan de la Costa, who was even now sobbing, 'My lovely boat! My lovely boat!'

---

[116] A dwarf in a biscuit tin.

'I'll get you another one,' said Our Hero. He never did. Neither did he ever pay Rodrigo de Triana or Martin Pinzon the bonuses he'd promised them for sighting land. Where were they anyway? How dare they go off like that without telling him!

Pinzon's ears must have been burning, because just then the *Pinta* appeared on the horizon. He was back, after two weeks away. And he'd found gold! He was instantly forgiven!

What a tale they would have to tell! What a welcome they would get!

A Sense of Achievement

Standing on the bridge of the *Nina*, which was carrying him home to Spain and glory, Cristóbal Colón reflected on his achievement. And what an achievement! Ha! Wouldn't those doubters look foolish when they realized that he'd been right and they'd been wrong! He'd done it! He'd discovered the Western passage to the Indies! They'd said it couldn't be done, and they were wrong.

Of course, they weren't wrong – he was. He hadn't discovered any western route to the Indies, but he had discovered something much, much bigger. America. Although it wasn't called that in those days.

Mind you, it wasn't anything like America as we know it. In those days McDonald didn't even have a farm, let alone an international chaim of Hamburger Retail Outlets. In fact, America had none of the wonderful things it has today, like Disney World, Hollywood, Madonna, TV Evangelists or New Kids On The Block. Colón's accidental discovery made all this possible. After all, without his intervention,

America would still be a nation of simple natives, smoking tea and hand-carving moccasins out of the jackets of potatoes.

It was Cristóbal Colón, and he alone, who dragged the American nation kicking, screaming, cheer-leading and ticker-taping into the twentieth century. Or at least he made it possible. You could say that it was all his fault! Not that he would have believed you. No. As far as he was concerned, he had discovered the Western passage and that was good enough for him. Certainly it was worth a hero's welcome, anyway.

Hail The Conquering Hero

Colón got the welcome he expected. The Catholic sovereigns did him proud. They threw a massive party at Barcelona in his honour. The only irritating thing about that was that the rest of the expedition had been invited too! He really could have done without them being there. Rude, uncouth fellows – not his type of person at all.[117] Still, he was the star of the show. And what a show!

There were the formal speeches, of course. Numerous dignitaries saying how brilliant he was. (Nothing he didn't know already.) Then there were messages of congratulation from other monarchs. Nothing from King John of Portugal. He was still insisting that the discoveries rightly belonged to him, as he'd been the first monarch to turn Colón down. You can't beat the Portuguese for logic, thought Cris as he sampled the vol-au-vents.

The Indians were a big hit. They were paraded in national costume, such as it was! Cristóbal couldn't

---

[117] Although many of them came from the same background as him.

help wishing that he'd insisted that they wore something ... er ... well, bigger! Still, they went down well
with the Queen!

After the usual jugglers, ordered specially since the
monarchs knew that Cristóbal was particularly
partial, there was dancing and a buffet. Never a great
dancer, Cris thought he'd just get a plate of twiglets,
then find a nice spot to pose and soak up all the
adulation. It was great being a hero. He could easily
get used to it. Uh-oh! Martin Pinzon was weaving
across the floor towards him! This was something Cris
could do without! Doubtless Pinzon was going to start
beefing on again about that stupid reward for spotting
land. Yes! All right! So he *had* said that Rodrigo de
Triana and Pinzon should get the prize. But he only
said it in a moment of excitement, didn't he? He
didn't really mean it, did he? And it was *his* expedition, wasn't it? They wouldn't even have been there
at all if it hadn't been for him, would they? No. He'd
been right to claim the prize for himself. Convincing
himself was one thing. Convincing Pinzon, who was
even now weaving towards him with a wine bottle in
his hand, was another. Colón demonstrated the
quickness of wit that had made him leader among
men – he dodged into another room.

It was a small ante-chamber, where the jugglers
were changing out of their stage costumes into
something even sillier. They barely looked up when
he entered. Could it be . . .? Yes! They didn't
recognize him! Hadn't the foggiest idea who he was,

148

and clearly didn't care. Typical theatricals! Don't want to know you unless they've seen you on the telly! At first he felt offended. Annoyed. Angry even. But then he rather enjoyed the anonymity. Enjoyed their company. Swapped old juggling stories.

'I bet you're a Leo,' said one of them, then offered to read his palm.

Why not? He already knew what his future held – enormous fame and vast fortune – but it couldn't hurt to have it confirmed.

The clairvoyant juggler gripped his fine hand in her leathery one and studied it with an expert, if jaundiced, eye. This is what she saw:

She saw him dying, soon. But first she saw him going on several journeys. Three big ones, then some little ones. Touching Colón for a handful of small change[118], she switched to the crystal ball. This is what she saw:

A second voyage of discovery, much bigger than the first. Seventeen ships and 1,200 men, all with their own hammocks probably. But this time the natives aren't so friendly. In fact, they're hostile. Perhaps the hawk bells have stopped working, or perhaps they've just had time to think about this bloke who came out of nowhere and started re-organizing and re-naming everything, when they were perfectly happy with the way things were in the first place – *and* insisting that they give him gold for doing it. It's hard to tell. The crystal's too cloudy to see. But she can see Colón

---

[118] From force of habit. She was too curious not to continue.

putting them down by force. Bloodshed. Some Spaniards are massacred. Colón is becoming obsessive. He's looking for gold. He shouts at them in Latin and all sorts of things. People are starting to complain, and it's not just the natives.

She decides not to tell him anything. Makes out the glass is too cloudy, the vibes aren't right. But after another handful of loose change she polishes the crystal and looks deeper into the future:

She sees a third voyage. Only six ships this time, and these are provided grudgingly. She sees Colón journeying south from La Isla Española[119]. She sees him reaching another landmass, and dismissing it as just another boring island. This landmass seems to be important, but the glass is cloudy[120]. The locals are really getting unfriendly. She sees chains, first on the natives and then on Colón. What does it mean?

A fourth voyage appears in the glass. There are only four ships now. He's going north. He appears to

---

[119] The place now referred to as Hispaniola.
[120] It *is* important. It's South America!

be ill[121]. He's being attacked by sharks, and by Indians.

She can't take any more. Placing her hankie over the crystal she tells him that he's going to have a long life, travel a lot, and have 75 children. Why tell him the truth? It'll only spoil his party.

Cristóbal Colón drifts back to the main room. He's missing all those people telling him how marvellous he is. Oh, good! Martin Pinzon is arguing with the king. With any luck they'll have him beheaded. He cannot possibly know that in just a couple of years Martin Pinzon will be dead and largely forgotten, although the people of Palos will erect a statue in his honour.

Queen Isabella is amused by the antics of the Indians. Someone has managed to convince her that

---

[121] He caught malaria.

what they're doing is an old New World custom. They do it all the time out there. She can't wait to visit! As Colón looks at her, he has no way of knowing that she will order him home from the New World in chains! Strip him of his governorship of Hispaniola, would you believe? And order him never to go near that island again! That's all the gratitude you get for shipping home slaves! Very soon she too will be dead.

Cristóbal Colón cannot know, as he acknowledges the nods of the friendly faces gathered in his honour, that over the next few years, in his lust for gold, by taking a wrong decision or a wrong turn, he will miss discovering Mexico with its untold Inca treasures and miss discovering the mainland of the New World, although he will go down in history as the discoverer.

He finds himself in conversation with another explorer. They seem to be coming out of the woodwork! This fellow's name is Amerigo Vespucci. Not in the same league as our Cris, naturally! But he confides in Colón that he would like to travel to the New World. As they take their leave of each other, Colón muses that if this Vespucci fellow ever discovers anywhere, they'll probably call it Amerigor, or Ameriga, or even America!

AMERIGO VESPUCCI

'America, Ha! What a ridiculous name!' he suddenly blurts out to a startled passer-by.

Home Again

Columbus retired to Seville. He was comfortably off but not particularly wealthy. His last two journeys had been failures, and he was largely forgotten. He felt bitter about being cheated out of many of the rewards promised by the king and queen and bitter about losing his governorship of Hispaniola.

'Huh! See if I care! I wouldn't be seen dead in that place anyway!'

Wrong again, Cris!

But no-one could take his achievement away from him. He had opened up a whole new world. Not many people could claim that.

He died in May 1506, and thus began a series of little journeys, possibly those seen by the clairvoyant juggler, but probably not.

He was buried in Seville.

Some years later his body was moved to Santo Domingo, on Hispaniola.

Two hundred years later his body was moved to Cuba, to keep it safe from the invading French.

In 1898 his body was moved back to Seville when Cuba obtained its independence. And there it stayed.

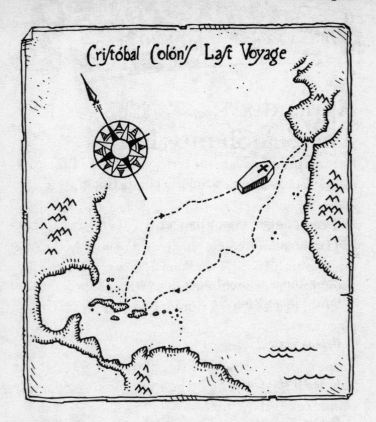

Cristóbal Colón's Last Voyage

Or did it?

Did it ever leave Seville in the first place?

Was it, as some people believe, someone else's body in the coffin?

Myself, I don't believe he's dead. *I saw* him only the other day, in a supermarket.

I knew him by the shoes.

Thick rubber soles.

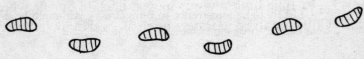

Appendix 1:
The Sea Shanty Lyrics

Here, as promised, are the lyrics of Colón's 1497 entry for the Eurovision Sea Shanty competition:

> Boom-banger, doom-danger,
> Tee-tanger, ding!
>
> Bong-binger, long-linger,
> Song-singer Bing[122]!
>
> *Repeat Verse Two*
>
> *Repeat Verse One*
>
> *Repeat Verse Two*
>
> *Jump In The Air And Shout 'Oi!'*

It's hard to understand why Spain doesn't win Eurovision more often.

---

[122] Unlikely to be a reference to Bing Crosby, although he did wear canvas shoes sometimes.

Appendix 2: The Other Two Ships And Their Crews

SANTA CLARA

This ship, otherwise known as the *Nina*, was even smaller than the *Santa Maria*. She was 55 feet long, and weighed 50 tons. Her crew[123] consisted of:

Captain: Vicente (Vince) Pinzon
Master:[124]   Juan (John) Nino
Pilot: Sancho (Sam) Ruiz de Gama
Surgeon:[125]   Maestre Alonso (Mr Alonso)
Marshal: Diego (Derek) Lorenzo
2 Petty Officers
8 Able Seamen
6 Gromets
Total crew: 21

THE PINTA[126]

Larger than the *Nina* but smaller than the *Santa Maria*, she weighed in at 60 tons and was 69 feet long.

---

[123] I don't know *their* weights!

[124] And owner.

[125] Really Mr Alonso was the ship's barber. They had been hoping to get Mr Roderick, who did a very nice demi-wave, but he was off work with a nasty swelling.

[126] The ship's nickname. More than likely in memory of that night in the Ferret and Spinnaker when Colón won the admiration of his crew.

Her crew were:

Captain:	Martín (Martin) Pinzon
Master:	Francisco (Frank) Pinzon
Pilot:	Cristóbal (Chris) Sarmiento
Marshal:	Juan (John) Reynal
Surgeon:	Maestre Diego (Mr Derek)[127]

2 Petty Officers
10 Able Seamen (including the owner, Cristóbal Quinter.)
8 Gromets.
Total crew: 27

Appendix 3:
The Crow's Nest

The crow's nest. Have you ever wondered how this strange item came about? Well, apparently in the early days of navigation, long before Cristóbal Colón even, there was a superstition about having crows aboard ship. They were meant to bring good luck by their very presence, just as an albatross was meant to bring bad luck. I think this latter has more to do with the fact that albatrosses are so huge that if you had one nesting up your mainsail, you'd find the ship almost impossible to move. But not so crows, which are a lot smaller.

---

[127] Another Barber. Mr Alonso suggested him for the voyage. In return Mr Derek gave Mr Alonso a recipe for quiche.

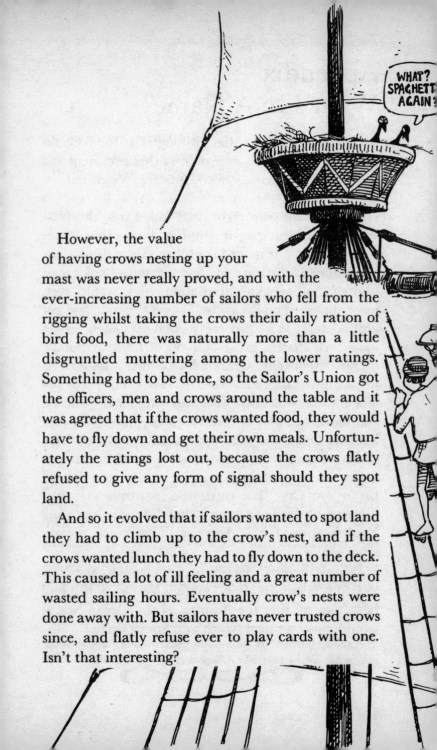

However, the value of having crows nesting up your mast was never really proved, and with the ever-increasing number of sailors who fell from the rigging whilst taking the crows their daily ration of bird food, there was naturally more than a little disgruntled muttering among the lower ratings. Something had to be done, so the Sailor's Union got the officers, men and crows around the table and it was agreed that if the crows wanted food, they would have to fly down and get their own meals. Unfortunately the ratings lost out, because the crows flatly refused to give any form of signal should they spot land.

And so it evolved that if sailors wanted to spot land they had to climb up to the crow's nest, and if the crows wanted lunch they had to fly down to the deck. This caused a lot of ill feeling and a great number of wasted sailing hours. Eventually crow's nests were done away with. But sailors have never trusted crows since, and flatly refuse ever to play cards with one. Isn't that interesting?

Appendix 4:
What's In A Name?

It's ironic, I suppose, that although Cristóbal Colón discovered America (more or less), that continent was named after somebody else – Amerigo Vespucci!

So who was this other fellow? Well, he was an explorer in his own right, had sailed into the New World and been instrumental in discovering Venezuela, but it was more his ability as a self-publicist that clinched the issue. He had written a book about himself, had songs written about him, would even have appeared on Breakfast Telly if someone had got around to inventing it early enough. Colón, as we have seen, had a great opinion of himself. But he didn't bother telling people how brilliant he was, he just assumed that they already knew. This, plus the fact that he was unpopular anyway, meant that he was soon forgotten, unlike Vespucci, who was a very likeable bloke and who kept in the public eye. He even managed to mix his dates around a bit, so that it appeared that he had arrived in the New World before our Cris! The rotter! So, naturally, when it came to thinking of a name, what did they plump for? You've guessed it – America. That's one theory, anyway.

I think there is a far simpler reason why the New World was named after Amerigo Vespucci. If it had been named after the Admiral of the Ocean Sea, it would now be called North and South Colón!